Walk with the Eagles
Hunting North American Big Game

Walk with the Eagles
Hunting North American Big Game

by
Doug Yajko

Foreword by Craig Boddington
Illustrated by William Davis

Roaring Fork Press
P. O. Box 563
Glenwood Springs, CO 81602
303-945-6533

For information, please contact:
Roaring Fork Press
P. O. Box 563
Glenwood Springs, CO 81602.

Although the author and publisher have made every effort to ensure the accuracy and completeness of information contained in this book, we assume no responsibility for errors, inaccuracies, omissions, or any inconsistency herein. Any slights of people, places or organizations are unintentional.

Printed and bound in the United States of America.

ISBN 0-9627247-6-9

LCCN 90-062139

ATTENTION HUNTING ORGANIZATIONS:
Quantity discounts are available on bulk purchases of this book for educational purposes or fund raising. Special books or book excerpts can also be created to fit specific needs. For information, please contact our Special Sales Department,
Roaring Fork Press, P.O. Box 563, Glenwood Springs, CO 81602

Or call (303) 945-6533.

Dedication

I want to dedicate this book to two members of the hunting community who have recently passed away. Both were 77 years old.

Roy E. Weatherby, creator of the famed Weatherby rifle, died April 5, 1988 following heart surgery. I first met Roy through some minor business dealings about seven years ago. He impressed me with his friendly manner and cheerful smile. He was honest to the letter—his handshake was his bond. After our deal had gone awry we remained friends and we continued to trade letters.

He honored me with invitations to his Weatherby Award Banquet three times in a row, and my picture appeared in the *Weatherby Guide*. He always returned my letters with thoughtful insight. He liked to hear from the younger hunting generation and sent me a copy of his first safari to Kenya in 1953. The price of the first elephant on that safari was $25 and the second was $15! To my constant amazement he answered my endless questions with forthright understanding. He always encouraged my active participation in conversations. He was a dedicated family man and pursued excellence in hunting and conservation.

John H. Batten passed away on February 15, 1989. Born in Chicago, the family moved to Racine, Wisconsin when he was three years old. After early schooling in Racine, he graduated from the Phillips Academy in Andover, Massachusetts. He continued his studies at the University of Wisconsin before starting to work at Twin Disc in 1935 as a factory trainee. By 1948 he was the company's president and CEO. Under his leadership Twin Disc became a multinational organization. Annual sales grew from $7 million to over $216 million and the company gained international recognition. He had two loves: flying and sheep hunting.

I met John at a party at the Foundation of North American Wild Sheep convention in Phoenix, Arizona. We talked of our schooling in New England. We also found we had sheep hunting as a common past time. He had taken most species of sheep in the world, while I was just a novice. Even so, he was more than willing to share his experiences with me. After returning home I sent him my copies of his books for him to autograph.

We started corresponding and he continually encouraged me to write of my hunting experiences. He encouraged me to put my experiences together in the form of a book. He critiqued the first three chapters of this book.

We always took time to discuss our most recent sheep hunt and traded pictures, at conventions through the years.

The hunting community and I will miss these two pillars in the years to come.

Acknowledgments

No one can collect and put together a journal of events without help. First I would like to thank my parents for *the right stuff.* Next I'd like to thank my family. The main theme came from the guides and outfitters, not only for guiding but for information about their areas and animals.

Next I would like to thank John Batten for the spark that ignited the idea behind the book. The transcribing and recopying of many chapters goes to my secretary, Peggy Sparks. The composition, layout, and general posture of the book is due to Marilyn and Tom Ross of About Books, Inc. This couldn't have been done without their help and assistance.

It was a privilege to have outdoor writer extraordinaire Craig Boddington of Petersen's Hunting to critique and write the foreword. His knowledge and technical ability led to some key ideas. Finally — and not the least — are the beautiful pen and ink drawings of master wildlife sculptor and artist William Davis of William Davis Wildlife Art, Cody, Wyoming.

Table of Contents

Foreword

It's easy to envy Doug Yajko. He discovered hunting at an early age, and has always lived where he could enjoy it readily—first as a boy in the Pennsylvania woods, then as an adult in the Colorado Rockies. Moreover, as a successful and highly respected surgeon, he has long been able to follow his hunting dreams to the far corners of this continent and beyond. Although Yajko's hunting experience spans several continents, it is his quests here in North America that form the framework of this volume.

From Alaska to Mexico, Pennsylvania to California, he has indeed done it all—and, yes, every reader of this work will wish he had been present on one or another of these hunts. Whether we have similar experiences in our won past or future, these hunting memories belong to Doug Yajko. We're fortunate he chose to share them, for you'll find his accounts honest, straightforward, and thoroughly enjoyable.

Many years ago, when I was a Marine lieutenant trying to sell some freelance hunting stories, a magazine editor who liked Marines called me into his office. In two hours he gave me a decade's worth of invaluable tips that have stayed with me to this day—but he also gave me a cryptic piece of advice that still haunts me.

"Boddington," he said, "you like to hunt; that's clear in your work. If you make a career out of writing about hunting you'll find it will ruin it for you."

How could that be, I wondered....

Today I know. I do indeed hunt a great deal, and I love it still. But I must do it under constant pressure. Deadline pressure, pressure to perform, pressure to have something to write about. Frequently, for that reason, there's the necessity to take an animal I'd prefer to pass in search of something better. And, indeed, pressure because a hunting writer really shouldn't miss, nor be too tired or in too poor shape to climb a mountain.

No, it hasn't ruined my hunting, and I wouldn't choose a different career path. But I can and do envy a man like Doug Yajko, who has the resources to hunt where he chooses — and does so for the very best reason of all: Because he enjoys it. It isn't his profession, nor is his hunting done from a need to compete with his fellows, nor in search of glory. It's his avocation, his lifelong hobby and pursuit that has led him to some of the grandest vistas on Earth. Within these pages you'll travel with him to the tops of the Rockies, the Cassiars, and the Brooks; to frozen tundras and scorching deserts; through forest and plain. You'll share his excitements and disappointments, and, as the author plainly has, you'll enjoy every tired, aching step.

For the serious hunter there is much value in this book. It is not a *how to,* yet contains much information on techniques and equipment that have worked. Nor is it a book of *where to,* though its readers will glean priceless information on worthwhile areas and outfitters. Its greatest value, however, is the sharing of the author's pure and simple pleasure in the sport and the wonderful country it has taken him to.

The sheer fun of it all comes through loud and clear. The clean satisfaction of bone-wearying effort, the taste of pure mountain air, the despair of failure that makes the thrill of ultimate success so sweet; the author understands these things, and understands, too, the hard work, patience, persistence, and the ability to take the bad with the good that our sport requires.

You'll get to know Doug Yajko quite well as you read his book. Over the years, I've rubbed elbows with him at hunters' conventions and Safari Club meetings, but I didn't really know him. Now, through these pages, I've backpacked with him into high alpine basins, I've closed with great bears, and I've waited for caribou that never came. In his writing he's as unassuming and modest as he is in person, but I've come to realize he's a tough, persistent hunter—and quite a nice guy besides.

Although I've been fortunate to spend a goodly time afield, there are hunts within these pages that I can only dream about making—and those dreams are enhanced by reading Yajko's accounts of them. On the other hand, he writes of several areas that my own hunting trails have led me into, and I could enjoy my own hunting memories while I enjoyed his. Most of us will experience this dual pleasure.

It was, for instance, with many a chuckle that I read of his first sojourn into northern Quebec for the caribou found there. Although in a different camp, I was there in that year of 1983 as well. I remember it as The Year The Migration Route Changed, the year the camps went from several seasons of near-perfect hunter success to near-zero. I got a caribou that year, a lone bull I slogged through 50 miles of tundra tussocks to find. Doug Yajko did not, though he tried twice. Nor did he succeed the following year. It's characteristic of him that he relates these disastrous hunts along with the fabulous ones, matter-of-factly and with no regrets nor indictments. Like I said, he's a nice guy...but with the determination that our sport demands, for he was back in Quebec the third year for yet another try!

The wonderful thing about that, and all the hunts in this book, is that it's clear and understood that he wanted the animal—but it's equally clear that just being there, enjoying the country and the game, was what it was all about, win or lose. So, in that spirit, sit back and enjoy one man's journeys to North America's great game field.

Craig Boddington, Editor
Petersen's HUNTING

Introduction

When we think of the good old sheep hunting days, the names of Jack O'Connor, Charles Sheldon, Herb Klein, Elgin Gates, John Batten, George Parker, and Theodore Roosevelt come to mind. Over the past two decades sheep enthusiasts have increased dramatically in number. The terms *Grand Slam* and *Super Slam* have become common.

In the old days a sheep hunt was six to twelve weeks long and bag limits were generous. However, there were few guides in the north country who could fulfill the clients needs.

Today the hunts are ten to fourteen days with frugal bag limits. There are multitudes of competent guides to meet sheep hunter's needs. What has not changed is the type of person who hunts sheep. Ovis pyrexia—sheep fever—becomes one of the strongest emotions known!

My North American Grand Slam started in the Northwest Territories and ended in Baja California. It took from August 1978 to January 1986 to complete. Along the way I've seen some of North America's most magnificent scenery. I've also made many good friends and had some unforgettable experiences.

I grew up in less scenic Natrona Heights, Pennsylvania—located on the Allegheny River, twenty-two miles north of Pittsburgh. The hills and gullies surrounding my home exited me more than the river. We didn't venture too far from home, but each weekend we traveled to Leechburg to see my father's family. The trip took us over the Allegheny River and through the countryside along both banks.

Life for me consisted of school, football and baseball, and growing up. The steel mills belched smoke over the valley. Summers were hot and sticky; winters were long and cold. I never considered these as inconveniences or concerns. Elvis was king and Truman and Eisenhower were presidents.

At the age of twelve, three events came to pass that made this book possible. I discovered golf, got my first shotgun, and dad bought a 52-acre farm. My eyes opened to the wonders of outdoors, and to the sport of hunting.

Small game hunting in Pennsylvania consisted of rabbits, pheasants, and groundhogs. We made one-day trips to locations where the extensive cover required a beagle to hunt successfully. Bag limits were tight and hunting was tough. I found a summer job as a caddie at the local golf course. This required early trips across the fairways were I could easily see tracks left the night before in the morning dew. Our farm was mostly woods, with the few open fields planted in pines to harvest as Christmas trees. It produced one of the finest whitetail deer habitats I have ever seen.

During this time my dad with his brothers shared a deer camp in northwestern Pennsylvania. Deer season always opened the first Monday after Thanksgiving. We looked forward to opening day with nervous anticipation. At age 14, our parents invited my cousin and I to go with them. We cut wood, swept floors, did dishes, and slept in crowded bunk beds—all for a few days of deer hunting. We could only reach the heavily wooded country around Kane, Pennsylvania by following logging roads and power lines on foot.

My first deer was a spike buck taken after lunch one cold day. We didn't return to camp for lunch so I started a fire to warm my hands and sandwich. It was so cold I left the fire burning very low. The smoke curled up across my stand by a large oak tree. I heard something coming. Through the trees wandered two does followed by a buck. The buck lifted his nose to smell the smoke and I had my first trophy. I'll always remember my elation and sense of accomplishment in those *foreign* surroundings.

After high school, I went to Washington and Jefferson College in southwestern Pennsylvania. Next came four years in Boston at Tufts Medical School and exposure to the northeastern terrain. New England was very beautiful but there wasn't time to enjoy the outdoors. During my years at W & J, I was president of my fraternity and the annual convention brought me to Boulder, Colorado. This was my first exposure to the west and the mountains. When it came time for internship I chose Denver to be close to the mountains and skiing.

Day trips to the mountains brought my first glimpses of mule deer, elk, and bighorn sheep. The plains were full of antelope and my heart once again turned to hunting. Although there was little time during residency for leisure, we managed a few trips for elk, deer, and antelope. These short sojourns brought me to some of the richest wildlife areas in Colorado. I borrowed my dad's prewar 30-06 and had a 4X scope mounted on it. Little was I to know that the distances were much longer in the west, but the animals looked closer due to the clear sky.

During those years it gave my dad an excuse to come west, and for the first time, personally experience the big country. Our excursions took us to the Flat Tops area of Colorado and names like Eagle, Meeker, Rifle, and Trappers Lake. The large distances between drainages thwarted us, and we hunted a different area each year with little success.

While we were having little or no luck, a friend of mine killed a trophy buck in Wyoming. Dad and I decided to try a guided hunt. My friend set it up and soon it was September. We headed for Afton, Wyoming for my first hunt off of horses. You can bet I found it quite an experience! At 4 A.M. we joined a farmer who was guiding during the day and farming at night. Hunting on the west side of the Wind River Range offers some of the most beautiful scenery in Wyoming. I saw three trophy size bucks, shot at two, and went home empty handed. This experience revealed the inadequacy of my distance recognition and shooting.

On the way home, we went through Jackson Hole and saw Yellowstone Park and the Tetons for the first time. Then we went to Douglas, Wyoming and both killed antelope. It was the first time I had asked to hunt on private land and to my surprise the farmer gladly gave permission.

During the next few years of my residency, I would head to the high country each fall and hunt with little success. I had mastered the art of hunting the antelope. Two trophies were taken in Wyoming at Lusk, and just north of Baggs, in Wild Horse Basin.

By now hunting had become an integral part of my fall vacation. I moved to practice in Glenwood Springs, Colorado — in the midst of some of the finest elk and mule deer hunting in the state. My practice soon became very busy and I had a trouble finding time to get away. A friend and I, after two years of futile high country camps due to weather and time restrictions, decided if we were to be successful we would have to go on a fully guided hunt in another area.

That started what will become the text of this book. The next eleven years included 25 different hunts in North America. These hunts consisted of trips to Alaska, Mexico, four provinces of Canada, and many of the contiguous states. They included all the huntable species of North America importable to the United States. This did not include hunts for the polar bear, walrus, or jaguar — none of which can enter the U.S. under the Marine Mammals Act and the Endangered Species Act.

Muskwa Country

By the end of the 1976 hunting season, I found myself thoroughly frustrated by my inability to get a trophy elk or mule deer. I had lived in Glenwood Springs, Colorado for three years and had hunted each fall, only to bag a small deer each year. I was familiar with the area in the White River National Forest but didn't have time for extensive scouting during the pre-season. Each year a friend and I found a good out of the way spot in the wilderness area. And each year it was overrun with hunters when the season started. We had no access to private land and found many exceptional trophies came from these areas.

Although my expanding surgical practice limited my time, I had bought a small gun store in town. The store received *Western Outdoors*, a hunting and fishing weekly. One week I noticed a small picture of a gentleman with a large six point bull. The caption stated he had been on a ten day hunt to northern British Columbia with Big Nine Outfitters. It also bragged he had seen sixteen five point bulls or better. I had hunted Colorado for seven years and had only seen one large bull from afar! I decided to better my chances and arrange a hunt in this area. Additionally, I wanted to bag species not available in Colorado.

I had no knowledge of the area or the type of hunting it offered. But I contacted Big Nine Outfitters and its owner Gary Powell. My letter brought a quick response. Not only did I find his area had elk but also moose, caribou, grizzly and black bear, Stone sheep, Rocky Mountain goat, wolf, and wolverine – thus the name, Big Nine Outfitters. The price of the hunt was quite steep. But, I decided if I could get three species during the ten day hunt it would be more than worth the money.

Gary explained I could take one species about every three days in good weather. My friend, Royal Smith, who had accompanied me on most of my Colorado hunts decided to go along. Royal wasn't interested in trophy quality animals, but he loved wild game. A chance to bring home some moose and caribou was all the excuse he needed. We scheduled the hunt for the last two weeks of September, during the height of the bugling season. We sent our deposits, got busy getting our licenses from Vancouver, and making plane reservations.

A trophy elk was my primary goal but the thought of moose and caribou was very inviting. Gary recommended we bring three or four boxes of shells and suggested we sight our rifles in at two hundred yards. I bought a .300 Weatherby earlier that year and spent a good deal of time sighting it in over the summer.

Finally September arrived and we were off to Denver to board a flight to Edmonton, Alberta. The size and beauty of Edmonton amazed us. This was to be one of many new and exciting experiences for me on this trip. After a restful night we boarded a Canadian Pacific Airways 737 and were off. We stopped at Grand Prairie and Fort St. John on our way to Fort Nelson. Fort Nelson is in the middle of the Omineca-Peace region of northern British Columbia.

We retrieved our bags and gun cases at Fort Nelson and made our way across the runway to a hanger with Valiant Air painted on the side. Although Gary was an experienced bush pilot with 4000 hours, his plane was not big enough to carry this load of hunters and gear. The charter service packed our gear and we met Tom Phillippe and his son Tom Phillippe Jr. who were also going to our camp.

I still remember my first ride in a noncommercial plane across Canada. We could see the hills in the distance as we headed out over low marshy areas. In twenty minutes we were over the hills and could observe the mountains rising toward the continental divide. The Rocky Mountains here have a valley floor about 1500 feet and the peaks are 8500 feet high. The mountain tops are round although many have steep ridges. Trees cover ninety percent of the terrain with a few open meadows along the rivers and on mountain tops.

Although Colorado has some big county, roads make most of it fairly accessible. I realized we hadn't seen a road or any other type of man made facility since we were a minute out of Fort Nelson. We descended, crossed a ridge, and the valley below us opened. A lodge and dirt landing strip waited in the distance. Soon we were on the ground and unloaded the plane.

To our surprise, four hunters boarded the plane for the trip back to Fort Nelson. We introduced ourselves and admired the four large elk racks, plus some moose and caribou racks on the ground. Shortly they were off and we settled into the beautiful lodge—each sharing a room.

Gary's main lodge is like a small settlement—complete with a generating plant, multiple wood cabins, fresh vegetable garden, and radio.

Pretty young cooks busied themselves making bread and cookies. Gary's wife, Olive, served a delicious dinner. Conversation centered on the itinerary for the next ten days. Gary told us to sight our rifles in early the next morning. Afterwards we would travel to a secondary camp about twelve miles down Gathto Creek.

That night we met our guides and received one pannier to be filled with only what we wanted at the next camp. We would leave the rest of our gear at base camp. The pannier measured 8" x 30" x 24" and one fit on either side of the horse. Like most first time hunters, I had enough gear to fill four panniers. I decided on extra underwear, socks, an extra pair of pants, and a wool shirt.

The 8 A.M. wake-up call surprised me, since I normally started much earlier on hunting days. We sighted our guns in and all hit the target at 100 yards. It took until mid morning to get the twenty-horse pack string together; then we were ready. We had four hunters, three guides, one cook, one wrangler, and supplies for ten days. The first day was fairly easy with only a six hour trip to the lower camp. There was a lot to learn.

I tied my rain gear on the back of the saddle, put my lunch in the saddlebags, and thought I was ready. Tom, Jr. and his dad wanted to hunt together so they shared a guide. Royal's guide was Omar Ginther who was about sixty years old and had lived most of his life in Eagle, Colorado. We had traveled 2500 miles to a wilderness hunting camp to find a guide who lived 25 miles away!

My guide, John Ferguson, was from Hudson Hope, B.C. where Gary lived in the winter. John decided not to follow the pack string down the river but to go one drainage north and parallel down to lower camp. About a mile out of camp, we left the area Gary had placed off limits so carcasses would not attract bears to the main camp. We turned north on a route that deteriorated from a well used bridle path to little more than a game trail. We went over a small pass and into the next basin and turned east to parallel the main river.

On the way to the floor of the basin we glassed the hillsides, soon spotting two large bull elk bugling in a high country meadow. They were a long way off but still looked impressive through binoculars. A little lower in the basin I saw my first band of Stone sheep. They disappeared into the dense over-growth as we settled down to have lunch.

"How about a moose on the first day?" asked John, pointing to a white spot about two-thirds of the way up the mountain. I calculated I had only eight and a half days to hunt since we would spend a day traveling back to base camp. I asked John about size and he said it was one of the biggest he'd seen this year. I figured with an allotment of one animal every three days, I'd have more time to concentrate on elk and caribou, if I took this guy now. It was the perfect time for elk but the caribou were not yet moving down from the high country.

"Why not?" I decided, and we were off. We left Royal with the horses to spot the moose while we climbed to outflank him. Our insulated vibram soles came in handy while crossing the valley floor to the cool north slope. The chilly early morning mist sharpened my senses. The hill was a lot steeper and the cover heavier than it looked from below. In about 45 minutes we figured we were at the right level, but couldn't see the moose. We determined he had fed to the right a little by watching Royal's hand signals through the binoculars. We made our way slowly along the hillside until we could see the large white horns. The jet black moose was facing away from us. The moose is North America's largest deer. This one was so close and so big, I could feel his presence.

As I hurried to shoot, John slowed me down. "The wind's right and as long as we're quiet he won't move. He's feeding." This surprised me because of previous requirements for split second decisions to shoot or not.

I caught my breath and sat down to rest my rifle on my knee. Against this huge, near black, golden antlered bull my .300 Weatherby, noted for it's punch, seemed inadequate. I took a deep breath, put the crosshairs behind his right shoulder, and squeezed the trigger.

The moose dropped like a rock. We approached the downed animal slowly, checking for any movement. There was none, so with difficulty, we positioned the animal for pictures. Then the work began. We caped and took the horns off first then removed the back straps and hind quarters.

I soon found a 1600-1800 pound moose on the ground provides
more exercise than I wanted in one afternoon.

We didn't find the bullet hole until we were right next to the base of the skull. I thought, "That's funny, since I placed the crosshairs behind the shoulder." But I shrugged it off as first day jitters.

After Royal arrived with the horses, we packed the quarters down the hill and put them in the top of a small tree. By then it was late afternoon and we still had a long way to go. We spent the next few hours winding down a narrow trail in a steep and narrow canyon. When we broke out into a flat area, I caught a glimpse of a large black bear. But by the time we got off the horses he had disappeared into the muskeg. We were crossing a muskeg flat when it started getting dark. Our horses jumped from one muskeg bush to the next. It was the only way they didn't sink in to their knees. In the fading light we couldn't avoid scratches and bruises to our knees when they lunged into the brush.

Wet and cold, we finally made it through a large wooded area to where we could see the camp lights. The lower Gathto Creek Camp had one cabin for hunters to sleep in. A second served as our kitchen and sleeping quarters for the guides. We hung up our wet clothes, had a fantastic meal, and headed for the sack. We learned to appreciate this hot evening meal as a marker to the end of each hunting day. A small wood stove dried the clothes overnight. Tom and Tom, Jr. had a leisurely trip down the river and were eager to head out for elk early the next morning.

Since we had left most of my moose in a tree, John decided we'd go back up the same trail, pick it up, and get it to the main camp. I didn't look forward to it but figured it couldn't be worse than the night before. The muskeg flat was frozen and made it a lot easier to cross that morning. We had just got into the steep part of the canyon when we found ourselves between two bugling bull elk. John started bugling back. He used no whistle, only his mouth and two fingers. To my surprise I saw a large six point bull slowly coming through the poplar thicket. He either saw or smelled the horses and stopped about seventy five yards away. We had already dismounted and were in position.

Talk about beginners luck, it was only the second day and I was about to take my second trophy. It wasn't to be. I lowered the crosshairs behind the shoulder and squeezed. The gun roared, the elk took two steps, and stopped.

"Settle down," John said softly, as I slowly put the crosshairs back a little right in the middle my trophy and squeezed. Again, the gun roared, the elk took two steps, and stopped.

"Something's wrong," I grumbled. "My gun must be off." I didn't want to just wound this beautiful animal, so we watched him slowly disappear into the poplar stand.

I was sick with disbelief over what had just happened. I couldn't hit the biggest elk I had ever seen within shooting range. The next six hours were pure emotional misery for me. As we made our way along the narrow path, I noticed the scabbard got banged fairly hard as we passed a tree. I had a big horse that couldn't negotiate the tight spots as cleanly as John's smaller mount.

Nothing had gotten to my moose. We loaded the quarters and the cape and horns on the extra pack horse and headed back to camp. On the way we spotted a big five point crossing Gathto Creek.

Back at camp we unloaded the meat. John set about cleaning and salting the cape and horns. I took the rifle to the porch and set up a bench rest. Gary had said to bring about 60 rounds of ammo and luckily I did. My first shot at one hundred yards missed the target. At twenty five yards the bullet barely caught the upper right hand corner of the three foot target. After another twenty rounds, I was back to three inches high at one hundred yards. A bore-sight would have saved many shots and a lot of noise.

Now I knew why the bullet hole in the moose was so far from where I had aimed. Luckily the moose had been facing the right direction and, although the bullet was off by about three feet, I was close enough to down it. The elk had been facing the other direction.

That night over a leisurely dinner I lamented my bad luck to Gary. He assured me I was not the first to have his gun knocked off during a ride. One must count on a certain amount of jarring the gun will take during a flight plus more in the scabbard on tight trails. From then on I protected the scabbard and the butt of the gun at tight spots in the trail.

Gary also reassured me there was still plenty of time and a *few* more six point elk in the mountains. I was hard to convince.

Up for a hearty breakfast the next morning, I met two new hunters from Australia. Bobby Grant and Carl Bartels had come to hunt elk and a few other species. They would fly to the mountain tops where they would spike camp and hunt down the sides.

By this time John had our horses saddled and we headed the twelve miles down Gathto Creek to the lower camp. About half way down we heard another bugling bull but couldn't coach it out to where we could see him. The heavy mist and the dense forest kept the bull well hidden. Farther down the main river basin we spotted our first mountain caribou. Three cows walked along the river basin toward the confluence of two mountain ranges.

We arrived in camp to find Royal, Tom, and Tom, Jr. not back from the days hunt. One by one they arrived empty handed. That evening Mike, the head guide, John, and Omar made plans for the next day. The rest of us talked about the vastness of the area and the amount of game it could support. Gary managed the area, only removing the oldest animals and leaving the younger to breed, thus assuring a continuing supply of trophy animals.

Controlled burns had turned dense forests into lush browsing areas for the game. I told my story about the six point elk and they countered with their sightings of good elk and moose. No one had seen a caribou yet but hopes were high.

After breakfast, we all took off in different directions. John chose to go back to Gathto Creek where we had bugled the elk the day before. Sure enough as soon as John bugled, he got an answer. It sounded very close. The bugling of the bull elk is a challenge from a bull without a harem. It is a declaration of rights and a warning given by the herd master to bulls who covet his cows. By now I needed no instructions to get off the horse and be ready. John stayed very close and soon we heard the elk approaching. It wouldn't come out in the open but finally, about sixty yards away, we saw a large eye staring at us through the brush. After *an eternity,* he moved slightly.

"He's a big one," John whispered. "I see ivory tips on his points."

It was an impressive set of ivory tipped horns, whitened from recent rubbing, glinting in the sun. I could see his shoulder since he was facing us. I put the crosshairs a little lower on the shoulder and squeezed. The gun roared. The elk whirled and galloped away. I was beside myself. John tried to settle me down by saying these large animals didn't always fall immediately. We went crashing through the muskeg kicking out a cow, calf, and small paddle bull moose.

We looked for blood and saw none. I assured John I was on the shoulder. I had made sure the gun hadn't been bumped again. We walked around in circles and still found no blood. John could see I was getting very upset. "I got an idea," John said, as he climbed a big tree to get a good view of the area. About half the leaves were off the trees and the visibility from his height advantage produced results. "He's over there about seventy five yards under a tree." I waited for John to get back on the ground, and we both ran to the spot he indicated.

The tines were long and rubbed pearly white during the rut.
There were no broken points—what a trophy!

I couldn't believe my eyes. There on the ground was a massive six point bull. I was elated. We took pictures and the work of caping and quartering began. We were so close to the main trail we took all the quarters and back straps along with the cape and horns. John's idea of bringing an extra pack horse paid off. We could pack all the meat and horns in one load.

Soon after we got back to camp Royal returned with the first caribou. Since he wanted the meat, he shot a young bull and had it skinned to tan the hide.

After dinner we waited for the other two hunters but finally gave up and went to bed. There was some concern, but since they were with the camp's main guide, Mickey, we figured they would be okay.

We had no sooner hit the sack, when the door crashed open and Tom and Tom, Jr. came in—tired, disheveled, and grinning from ear to ear. They had stalked what they thought was one bull, only to find there were actually three together. They both dropped prime bulls. Their excitement was contagious. We had a party celebrating the day's take. We all knew no matter what else happened the hunt was already a success.

We left a little later the next morning, due to all the cape preparation and meat hanging. Royal, Tom, and Tom, Jr. took the day off. John and I decided to ride to a caribou crossing on one of the smaller creeks. We had just set up a small blind on the bank when it started to rain. We put on our rain gear and sat under the lean to all afternoon only seeing one cow caribou. The sky cleared about dusk as we headed toward camp. We set up the spotting scope to glass nearby ridges. We saw three caribou cows heading over a ridge.

The next day John and I decided to go higher to look for caribou. Royal, Tom and Tom, Jr. went to *the moose pasture* where it was not unusual to find quite a few moose. We crossed Gathto Creek and headed uphill. A couple of hours later, we broke out of the trees and headed for the top of the mountain. It was a grassy knoll where we could sit and see forever. Gathto Creek looked like a small snake crawling along the valley floor. John told me the caribou liked to stay high to avoid flies and keep cool, this time of year. We looked through our binoculars all day before returning to camp for the evening meal.

We found Royal, Tom, and Tom, Jr. already there and the air filled with excitement. All three had killed moose and Royal had come very close to a grizzly bear. Royal had killed a smaller bull for the meat. The two Tom's had each downed a big moose. We had a grand dinner and spent hours retelling the day's events. Gary flew in and joined us for dinner on his way to base camp. The hunt pleased him very much.

The next day Royal and the Toms went to bring their moose to camp. John and I went back to the area close to where I had downed the elk. There was a bench about five hundred yards from the creek and high enough to afford a commanding view. We tied the horses in a nearby poplar stand and found an open spot to glass. After about an hour, John went to get our lunches. No sooner had he returned when we spotted caribou coming into the river bed.

He glanced quickly at them and said, "Let's eat; they're all cows."

After a few bites, I took another look. "John, the body of the last one is twice as big as the others." I set up a spotting scope and settled down to scrutinize the tail gunner. They methodically made their way down the river toward us. Finally, they turned so I could see the horns in the light.

John exclaimed, "Let's go! We'll try to get to the river before he gets to us."

About two hundred yards from the river, I spotted a small grove of pine trees to hide in. I thought I'd die as we sprinted down the hill and through the brush to get to them. As we reached the grove, I was badly winded. I sat down behind a log to use for a rest as the first cow caribou appeared. Slowly, they made their way down river in single file. By the time the bull arrived I had caught my breath and was ready. His white mane and palmated horns were impressive. I waited until he was broadside and put the crosshairs on his shoulder. The first bullet staggered the animal; the second put him down for good.

For me the celebration started for real! All the pressure of the first hunt was behind me. I had never been happier. In only seven days I had killed trophy elk, moose, and caribou.

The picture we took there on the creekbed later appeared in the *Weatherby Guide*. The size of my smile probably convinced them to print it. After caping and quartering my latest trophy, we headed back to camp for a *real* celebration.

Tom and Tom, Jr. were packing to leave—they were out of tags! I still had grizzly and black bear tags, but only planned

The bull was a good Osborn Mountain caribou
with large palmated antlers.

to use them if we spotted one by chance. Tom and Tom, Jr. headed out to make the next day's flight. Royal and I relaxed and enjoyed the time away from our busy practices. Royal went fishing and caught a few Dolly-Varden and grayling. I watched John finish caping the caribou and salting it and the skull. The guides that worked for Gary took pride in all aspects of their work. Later that afternoon, we headed back to the main camp arriving very tired.

Both the elk and caribou horns impressed Gary. He said they were the largest taken this year. Royal and I packed quickly when Gary told us we could get to Fort Nelson by evening. Bobby Grant returned with an elk and a moose on the ground. Carl was still in the field but had taken a moose. He also bagged a black bear with a long shot even his guide couldn't believe.

We swapped stories of down under and of their trips to Africa before we left. Valiant Air was on time, so we bid goodbye to Gary, Olive, John, Omar, and the rest the crew, and headed for Fort Nelson.

We made straight for a motel and a long hot shower. A big steak dinner topped off the evening. And a bed with a mattress was a pure delight. The next day we had our meat processed and wrapped for shipping. Gary would send the capes and horns at the end of the season.

We boarded the CP Air 737 and headed home. At our first stop, Fort St. John, Tom, and Tom, Jr. boarded. Our renewed camp-like atmosphere made the journey to Edmonton more fun. We stayed overnight in Edmonton, had another celebration dinner—this time for Tom, Jr. who was going home to Indianapolis to get married. He was going on a Montana antelope hunt for his honeymoon. I learned he had taken a large Boone and Crockett woodland caribou in Newfoundland the year before.

Next morning we said our goodbyes and headed for Denver. The flight was long, but gave us time to reflect on our ten days in the wonderful area Gary managed. It is about forty miles wide by a hundred and fifty miles long, bordered on the south by the Muskwa River and on the north by a ridge of mountains. The eastern border is the Alaskan Highway and the west is the continental divide.

**This beautiful area contains some of the greatest
game populations in North America.**

I couldn't believe how lucky I was to find Gary on my first
hunt. I often long to return to Gathto Creek and the base
lodge set in hunter's paradise.

Mountain caribou

2

Arctic Red River – My First Sheep

Still elated from my successful hunt to British Columbia, I started looking for next year's hunt. Tom Collinson, the editor of the *Glenwood Post* told me about Skip Quade, a friend of his in Hutchinson, Minnesota who planned to hunt Dall sheep in the Northwest Territories. When I contacted him he gladly gave me the name of Ray Woodward of Arctic Red River Outfitters.

I contacted Ray to get information about the hunt. It was scheduled for the end of August. He had hunted that part of the country only one year and was still familiarizing himself with the area and terrain. He had taken six Dall sheep the year before – one for each hunter, plus two grizzlies. The idea of getting a bear as a bonus was very inviting. Shortly after Christmas, Skip called to tell me they only had three in their party and had room for one more. I had checked out Ray's references and knew if there was an opening I wanted to fill it. As soon as I said yes, my thoughts once again turned to the north. This hunt would be different, since we would fly in and then backpack to the hunting area. I had back-packed some overnight trips but never had spent five days in a spike camp.

I sent my deposit and confirmed the dates of August 20th through September 2nd. Because I was a novice at sheep hunting I started reading everything I could find about the subject. When sheep hunting talk starts, the first name that comes up is O'Connor. I read as many books and stories as my evenings allowed prior to the hunt. It became clear the most important part of the hunt would be the stalk. During the stalk wind direction, noise, and smell would come into play. In the open country habitat of this animal all these things are important considerations. It excited me just to think about the stalk.

In preparation I found the rosewood fore-end of my rifle had cracked the year before at Gary's. I sent it back to Weatherby for a replacement. My gun arrived in late spring and eagerly set about sighting it throughout the summer. The shot could be much longer than any of the previous year. I wanted to make sure the Weatherby was on. I couldn't handle a repeat of the previous year's frustration!

At times it seemed August would never come. But soon enough I was on the plane to Edmonton. Once again, I spent a pleasant day there before heading north. The trip took us to Yellowknife, capital of western Northwest Territories, and on to Inuvik, high above the Arctic Circle. After we crossed Great Bear Lake and Great Slave Lake, we turned south and landed at Norman Wells. Yellowknife was larger than I had expected. It was much bigger than Fort Nelson. Norman Wells consisted of a main street and a few streets around it with houses.

Norman Wells was a refinery established about the turn of the century. It had grown into the commerce center for the middle MacKenzie Valley. A van from the Norwel Inn met us when we landed. We found the Inn quite comfortable. We settled in and busied ourselves with seeing the town. It was on the banks of the large MacKenzie River. The MacKenzie starts at Lake Athabasca and is one of the few rivers in North America which flows north and empties into the Arctic Ocean. The river is three miles wide at Norman Wells and freezes solid in the winter and becomes "Mackenzie Bridge." There are no roads north or south from Norman Wells. Barges and airplanes are the only modes of transportation.

I had my first look at permafrost housing. Everything sits above the ground, including all the utilities. Government sponsored housing was available to most of the townspeople and employees of the refinery. We went to the Royal Canadian Mounted Police (R.C.M.P.) and purchased our hunting licenses. They told us we would get our tags after the hunt. We also got some good news. There were no trophy fees for the species we were hunting. Skip, H.P., and Homer went fishing and brought home some six to eight pound lake trout that would taste wonderful between backpack meals.

We contacted Perry Linton of Nahanni Ltd. and made arrangements for the next day's trip to Goober Lake. Nahanni is Indian for beautiful valley. We went back to the Norwel and had a great dinner fixed by the owner, Leo Hardy. Skip and I were in good shape but his dad, H.P., and Homer were well into their sixties. We were concerned how they would hold up under the strain of a backpack hunt. We found out later, Ray was way ahead of us in planning for the elderly gentlemen. That night we sat on the deck of the Norwel Inn reading the newspaper until midnight. It was still daylight.

Perry picked us up about ten the next morning and drove us to a small lake south of town. There was the high performance Beaver that would fly us to Goober Lake. We loaded all our gear, pushed away from the dock, and headed to the middle of the lake. It was a little choppy but long enough for an easy takeoff. As we turned west we crossed the mighty MacKenzie. it looked even larger from the air. How could it freeze solid in October and stay frozen until late May? A new highway was under construction between Whitehorse and Inuvik. When finished, the Dempster Highway would need ferry service across the MacKenzie in the summer but could cross the *bridge* during the winter months.

Across the river was a landing strip for materials needed by the mining exploration going on in the mountains. Our first sights were familiar swampy areas which soon gave way to much steeper hills devoid of trees. The only green was within one hundred yards of the streambed. We headed west for the Yukon border situated in the middle of the MacKenzie Mountains.

Just this side of the border we flew over a high mountain pass where we could see a small lake with two large wall tents on the banks. As we turned we could see rivers running east-west from the lake. Turning sharply, we were soon splashing to a stop on the lake's surface. We taxied to shore where a hulk of a man, Ray Woodward, greeted us. Ray stands close to six feet six inches, weighs around 220 pounds, without an ounce of fat on his frame. The newly moved camp was still under construction. We carried our gear to our sleeping tent and said goodbye to Perry. He would return in ten days to pick us up.

The main camp on the bank of Goober Lake

Perry taxied to the far end of the lake, revved his engine, and barely cleared the other end of the lake. I wondered if he would have made it with our load on board. It was a beautiful blue sky day and the lake was crystal clear. The peaks around the pass were eight hundred to a thousand feet high charcoal gray. There was not a tree in sight. Nonetheless the view in all directions was spectacular. Though it was seven p.m. we had plenty of time to store our gear and meet Ray, Barry, and Gabe—our outfitting team. As part owners in the area Ray and Barry had a vested interest in making our stay successful.

Ray showed us around, then we sat down over a cup of hot coffee. He explained that he and Barry would guide H.P. and George from the base camp. Gabe, an Indian guide, would take Skip and I to spike camp a few days from base camp. Skip unpacked his fishing rod and headed for the lake to catch dinner. I got my binoculars and glassed the surrounding mountains for sheep.

It was a beautiful day and the lake was crystal clear. The peaks around the pass were eight hundred to a thousand feet high charcoal gray.

After a dinner of Skip's fish and fried potatoes we mapped out the next day's events. Skip and I were to pack for two to four days. This meant one dry change of clothes, rain gear, food, and sleeping bag. Gabe had a bad back but had brought along two of his dogs, King and Sport, to act as a pack team. These two huskies carried all the food and our tents. We hit the sack early knowing the next day would be a long one.

I shouldered my forty pound pack and we headed east up the valley. The two valleys faced east toward the MacKenzie. When we got to the top of the pass, the two valleys became one. Skip and I headed down it. Ray took H.P. around to a small side valley where he had spotted a band of rams. Gabe led us down to the valley floor which was surprisingly easy walking. My Herman Survivors again proved a good investment for my feet. They had held up well the year before in B.C. We took our shoes off to cross the stream that wandered through the valley floor. In August the stream was only twenty feet wide but you could see where it marked the bank during the high spring runoff.

The mountains looked much higher from the valley floor. We headed east. After about three hours we came to a spot where a small stream came tumbling out of the rocks and ran into the main stream. We stopped, made camp, and had lunch. After lunch we followed the small stream up into a smaller valley. Here we stopped to glass. To my surprise we spotted some twenty rams in three different bands. We sat down to let the sheep settle. There were rams everywhere. We spotted three big ones high up to the west, a group of younger rams in the valley floor, and five large ones feeding away from us.

Gabe didn't tell me what he wanted to do. After fifteen minutes I thought it was time to move. I motioned to him and Skip to move up to take a look at the band feeding around the corner. There was nothing between the rams and us but air. A stalk was impossible. The closest ram had a badly broomed off horn. As we glassed the five feeding around the corner the smaller rams in the valley spooked.

Suddenly all the rams disappeared. I learned quickly that too many sheep made it hard to get close to any of them. Gabe explained later he had wanted the larger rams to feed out of sight before we moved. We followed the sheep, but as we rounded the corner they topped out over the next ridge.

We watched in awe as the sheep traversed a sixty degree slope without breaking stride. Gabe spotted five white specks above us. We climbed the sixty degree slope and gained real appreciation of the sheep's feat! After two hours of climbing, we were about fifty yards underneath the sheep. They were bedded down. I had read how to judge a ram's horns. After twenty minutes Gabe and I agreed the largest was only thirty six inches. Disappointed, we headed toward the valley to our tent and dinner.

Next morning I found walking on the rocks had taken its toll. My feet had swollen badly. I crawled out of the sleeping bag to see Gabe had the spotting scope set up and was looking for sheep. He had located a band of three rams about two miles away in a small basin. After a backpack breakfast and more glassing, we broke camp and headed east. We walked all day to where some small pines nestled at the confluence of two streams. It looked like an ideal place to camp. As we made camp and cut wood for the fire I noticed a single ram feeding about five hundred yards away. I set up the scope and checked the wide sweeping curve to his horn, and how high his horn went above the bridge of his nose. His right horn had been broomed off slightly. But he was still a magnificent trophy.

I challenged Gabe, "Get me in position and I'll take him." He was feeding away from us. More importantly, a rock outcropping about one hundred yards above him provided a great vantage point if we could get to it without spooking the ram. It was five o'clock, but the sun was high and plenty of daylight remained. We took off at ninety degrees from the sheep, up a steep narrow valley with a small bubbling stream. Soon we were out of sight of the sheep. We made our way slowly up the steep side to the rock outcropping.

I was breathing hard as we neared the top. Gabe stopped, sat down, and lit a cigarette. I couldn't believe it. I was ten feet from a clear view of the sheep and my guide wanted a cigarette! I didn't know the smoke would confirm the wind drift, and wouldn't bother the game. By the time he had finished, my heart rate had slowed considerably. He checked to be sure I was ready and had loaded my gun. I crept over the edge but couldn't spot the ram.

I finally spotted him in a small depression in the side of the mountain about a hundred yards below. He had bedded down and was gazing out over the valley. I checked again to make sure this was the same sheep. I put the crosshairs on his back, squeezed. He never got out of bed. When we got to the sheep, he was larger than we thought. In the excitement we. forgot our tape, but he was an old ram with heavy bases and a true trophy. Gabe explained this would have been his last year. His teeth were bad, and he had little body fat to get through the harsh winter.

It was now eleven o'clock and getting dark. Gabe quickly caped and quartered the ram. We took as much as we could back to camp. By the time we got back it was close to dark. Skip had a fire going and all offered their congratulations.

The tape showed the ram to have fourteen inch bases and a length of thirty-nine and three quarters. It scored 164 Boone and Crockett. The growth rings on the ram showed he was thirteen years old. My first ram was a dandy! I was quite proud of the accomplishment that came from hard effort. Instead of backpack food that night we had tenderloin of ram. Red meat never tasted better. Gabe said he was sure he had seen a ram on the back of Ray's packboard as he ascended the hill back to camp the day before.

So H.P. had his ram—we had only two more to go. Gabe quickly constructed a shelter for our heads and gear in case it rained. This Indian really knew how to live in the woods. I plopped my head down in the sleeping bag completely exhausted.

The next day we loaded the cape and horns on my pack, which upped the weight to nearly seventy pounds, and headed for base camp.

King and Sport carried the heavy meat.
I really appreciated the dogs now.

A great trophy—but this would
have been his last year.

We covered two day's walk in one day. It was all up hill. We stopped at eleven for tea. It amazed me Gabe only took five minutes to make a fire and start tea. The dogs were hot and laid down in the shallow stream to cool their bellies. Gabe talked about growing up on the banks of Great Slave Lake. He told of hunting and fishing for subsistence. He would leave after the next hunt to fish for whitefish to supply his dog team with food for the long winter. He spent winters on the trap line. It was important to have well fed dogs. Gabe had only been out of the area once when he went to Inuvik to have back surgery. He had a son who went to school in Inuvik, and only made it home every six weeks or so.

The sky was darkening and it looked like rain. It started as we approached our final climb to the pass. The seventy pounds felt like five hundred; each step hurt. We topped the hill and spotted the tents. Our pace picked up and we were soon at the door of the wall tent. Ray was very proud of our trophy. The size of the rams bases impressed him. His horns were also darker than usual for this area.

After dinner we collapsed into our sleeping bags and fell asleep to the sound of rain on our tents. We awoke the next morning to find eighteen inches of snow on the ground. Snow shouldn't be on the ground on August 26th. Spotting white sheep against white snow is extremely tough. So we spent the day playing cards and talking about bear. The previous hunt bagged two grizzlies but there were none seen this hunt. H.P. and Homer decided to take a few days off and fish. They were pooped.

The next day Skip, Gabe, and the pack dogs again headed east to look for sheep. Ray and I climbed to the head of a high mountain pass and glassed for caribou and bear. We saw sheep in all directions but no moose other than a cow. Ray, who spent his winters in southern Alberta running a propane distributorship, told me his area consisted of seven thousand square miles—some of which he hadn't yet seen. He planned to move the camp for every four sheep hunters this year to get more familiar with the area. He told me about growing up in southern Alberta and hunting bighorn sheep. Finally in the late afternoon Ray spotted a grizzly bear. It was quite a thrill to see my first grizzly even though it was a sow with cubs.

We awoke the next morning to find eighteen inches of snow on the ground. Snow shouldn't be on the ground on August 26th!

Back at camp H.P. and Homer were rejuvenated. Ray made plans to take Homer in another direction for his sheep. I rested and played cook the next day. Skip and Gabe returned about mid day with a full curl ram. They had climbed into the basin where we had taken the largest ram a few days before. Ray and Homer returned without having seen a ram close enough to stalk. That night we made plans to head west and a little lower to look for bear. Ray stayed at base camp with George to get his sheep.

We packed west to the head of a long valley and descended to the floor. We walked all day to a confluence which was the head waters of the Arctic Red River. We made camp and scouted a few of the small basins off the main valley floor. Once again we found Dall sheep everywhere. We photographed them on sheer cliffs and grazing in open terrain. Next morning we looked for bear, again to no avail. Although the snow had melted, Gabe thought it might move the game a little.

The next morning we headed back to base camp. Again, it was all uphill but this time no one carried any extra baggage. On our arrival, we were delighted to learn Homer had killed a ram the previous evening and Ray was out packing it back. Ray returned with another full curl ram. We decided to have a party. Of course, in the middle of the MacKenzie Mountains with only Coleman stoves for heat and light it was a subdued party. The fresh fish that H.P. and Homer had caught before we made our way to Goober Lake tasted wonderful.

**Ray had done a masterful job of getting four full curl rams
in eight days—especially since two were taken by gentlemen
in their late sixties.**

Next morning we packed and waited for Perry to pick us up. Ray had contacted him on the radio and the weather was good enough to fly. We heard the Beaver before we saw it. He made the same turn over the west end and was quickly on the lake. He taxied in and dropped off the last four hunters of the season. We loaded up and headed out. This time Perry revved it hard and long, before taking off. We barely cleared the end of the lake. Once airborne I relaxed. The ride to Norman Wells retraced our trip in and went smoothly. The Norwel was full so Perry arranged for a van from the MacKenzie Mountain Lodge to pick us up. A hot shower felt sooo good and sleep came easy after our large steak dinner.

Next morning we checked our sheep with the R.C.M.P. for measuring and pulling a tooth. We repacked our gear and waited for the plane from Inuvik. The ride to Edmonton was long but the thoughts of mountains so plentiful with white sheep made it easy. Skip, H.P., and George made connections to Minneapolis but I had to lay over in Edmonton. Next day I headed for Denver and on to Glenwood Springs. The aspen had started to turn and were beautiful in their golden splendor.

Barren ground caribou

3

Return to Muskwa Country

Planning next year's hunt was exciting because I had contracted Ovis Pyrexia. This sheep fever comes in many forms and mine created an ingrained longing for the tops of mountains and the animal that roams there. One sheep hunt had fixed my mind with a desire to continue to pursue these wonderful creatures. The population of Dall sheep is approximately one hundred thousand spread across the top of North America. Alaska, the Yukon, and the Northwest Territories contain excellent huntable populations.

Sixteen thousand five hundred Stone sheep exist in one small pocket of British Columbia. The southern border is the Peace River and the northern the Yukon border. Gary Powell's Big Nine Outfitters is right in the middle of this area. When L. S. Chadwick went out for meat and returned with a ram measuring fifty two and one-eighth along the outside curl, the Muskwa country became the premier location for Stone sheep. I made the decision easily after seeing all the full curl rams lying on the floor of Gary's meat shack. He also had the most Stone sheep permits in northwestern British Columbia.

I wrote Gary and scheduled dates for the last two weeks of September. He was full at that time but said since I had been there before he would add me as the fifth sheep hunter. It was to be a one-on-one hunt in a different area than I hunted before. I can't describe my excitement about my return to this paradise in northern B.C. I wanted to take a Rocky Mountain goat if at all possible. Gary thought it should work out fine. I sent my deposit and busied myself reading more about sheep hunting and specifically about Stone sheep.

September finally arrived and I headed north to Edmonton, once again. Canadian Pacific Airways retraced my former route through Grand Prairie, Fort St. John, and on to Fort Nelson. I rounded up the hunters going to Gary's and lead them to Valiant Air. We landed at base camp and unloaded the gear. Gary's main camp is a lodge with all the extras: heat, electricity, generator, hot showers, and home cooked meals with <u>more</u> than you can eat.

The ride in was as beautiful as before. The leaves were just starting to turn and the hillsides were ablaze with color.

We got situated and learned that a physician from Texas and his friend would go to one spike camp. The other three of us would head toward the continental divide. A lawyer, Bill Gumble, who had hunted with Gary before and taken a thirty four inch sheep, had returned to find a larger one. Jack Drytkes, a rancher from Wyoming, was our third member. We learned that there was one day left in caribou season. The shorter season was due to heavy kills by predating wolves.

Two in the party had caribou tags and wanted to hunt the final day. Early in the morning they took off for the high country to try to find a trophy. Two wanted to rest at base camp. After Gary introduced my guide, Carl Vig, I wanted to go for a horseback ride to toughen up a little. We packed nothing because we intended to return to base camp by evening. Carl knew a small basin where rams sometimes hide when hunting pressure was high. He figured we could get to it by midday.

I wanted to go for a horseback ride to toughen up a little.

An hour out of camp we crossed a rain swollen upper Gathto Creek and headed into the small basin. We came across a winter kill ram of four or five years as soon as we crossed the stream. The wolves and the porcupines had left little waste. Next we encountered a cow moose with it's calf and skirted it with caution. I got a chance to use my new telephoto lens and got a great picture. Leading our horses about two hundred yards above the creek bed, we topped out on the first bench, and spotted a white object through the small trees. It was feeding two hundred yards above. I knew Dall sheep didn't range this far south so this must be a Rocky Mountain goat.

Carl tied the horses, and set up the scope. To our surprise it was a lone billy feeding in an area not characteristically steep and rocky. It looked like a small one, and I didn't want to shoot it this early in the hunt.

This brings up the problem of judging an animal when it is alone. O'Connor said if the horns were as long as the length from the tip of the nose to the eye it was a trophy. The goat was feeding slowly and the wind was right, so we had plenty of time to check him out.

I had read goats were very tough and that it took a heavy load to bring them down. Occasionally they jumped off high precipices when hit. We decided to take the animal. Carl made a rest on his shoulder in front of me since it was about a sixty degree angle uphill. I put the cross hairs behind the front shoulder and squeezed. The goat only flinched, so I fired again. This time the animal disappeared. We could see the side of the hill but no billy. He must be heading toward a rock face. If he crossed it he would come out in the open. We waited. Nothing moved. Carl thought the second shot had dropped him but we wanted to be safe. Shooting uphill is always difficult.

Rocky Mountain goats are sturdy, compact animals. A large male stands forty inches high at the shoulder and measures five to six feet in length. Both males and females have blackish needle sharp horns. They join the Dall sheep and polar bear as one of three North American species that are white all year. Estimated populations are between twelve to fifteen thousand in Alaska, forty five thousand in British Columbia, seven thousand in Montana and Washington, twenty five hundred in Idaho, and one thousand in Yukon Territories. Also small populations roam in Alberta, Colorado, South Dakota, and Wyoming.

We started to climb and soon found why we couldn't see the animal. There were little benches and shelf-like areas where an animal could lie unnoticed forever. Thirty minutes later, we still hadn't found the kill. Finally using the tethered horses as a spot, we found the goat lying on one of the benches. He had jet black horns and snow white hair. He sported a well developed beard and long hair on his chaps. Carl had learned a new way to skin the animal down the back for a life size mount. He tried it since I wanted the goat mounted this way. His shorter than estimated skull fooled us.

The horns measured eight and one-half inches, a respectable goat but not as good as we thought.

I still had twelve full days to hunt sheep. My excitement showed. Although I had a grizzly tag, very few were spotted in the area. We made our way up the hill and into the small basin but found no rams. We headed back to camp, where Carl cleaned and finished off the cape while I packed for our next trip. The cape was bloody, but I learned a trick that cleaned it. We soaked the cape in a fast running small stream overnight and the next day it was clean.

Once again too much gear had to go in one pannier. Our pack string consisted of a cook, horse wrangler, three guides, three hunters, and fourteen horses.

Chester returned without a caribou but Peyton had a very respectable one. Bill had passed on a thirty six inch ram. Gary, Bill, Jack, and I discussed our next hunt. Gary said we would be at the highest part of his area close to the continental divide. He told us his former partner Don Peck's area bordered it to the north. Olive fixed a hearty, satisfying dinner and we went to bed thinking about our trip next morning.

We packed the horses in the early rain and were under way by ten A.M. It wasn't long before we had our first wreck. A wreck or blowup occurs when one or more of the horses decide to lay down under their load or buck it off. It requires a great deal of patience and skill to handle the stubborn animals when this happens.

The drizzle stopped as we finished repacking some of the horses. We could finally remove our rain gear. Eight miles up Gathto Creek it forks. We took the west fork up a steep hill and along a sheer overlook. We continued west and descended into the valley floor. The steep valley sides and timber mixed with rock slides made hunting very difficult.

Ten miles further we came to a flat area under some large pine trees where the drainage once again divided. We made camp here. The guides and horse wrangler set up the cook tent for the female cook. Then they set up the guides and hunter's tents, cut fire wood, and hobbled the horses. The camp was ready—complete with wood stove to make fresh bread, hot rolls, and hot meals after a long day's hunt.

Sleep came quickly that night after the long ride. It felt like I had just fallen asleep when I heard the wrangler chasing the horses. It was time to get up for breakfast already! During breakfast Jack, Bill, and the guides decided to go north into a sheltered basin that rams frequented. Carl and I choose to go west toward the divide. A mile out of camp we spotted nine rams feeding slowly toward a steep basin. We figured they had been to water and were working their way back to higher ground. Carl decided two or three of them were worth a closer look. We found no way to approach them from below so we moved one basin west and climbed a steep wall to get around and above them.

The going was tough, and Carl had to slow down for me to keep up with him. The steep wall of the basin opened up and the ascent became much easier along one side. I was told no one could keep up with Carl. Soon I believed it. His six foot two frame carried about a hundred and sixty pounds of muscle. He never even breathed hard. He was a classic cowboy and prided himself in the off season by bronc riding. I fell back to about fifty yards behind him but he slowed as we reached the top.

We crept over the top to a small outcropping about twenty yards down where we set up our spotting scope. I made a classic error of leaving my gun ten feet away. The rams were four hundred yards below us, feeding uphill.

As the day warmed the wind began to swirl and the rams fed to within about one hundred and fifty yards. Carl estimated the largest sheep would go thirty eight but was quite heavy. I hesitated because I was looking for that forty-incher and I had plenty of time left in the hunt. I took some exciting photos with my telephoto lens. Carl finally convinced me there were very few sheep in this area any larger. Finally, I decided to take him.

Now not keeping my gun beside me, came back to haunt me. The sheep had fed up close where they would see any movement. I tried to roll slowly to the right to get my gun.

Carl whispered, "freeze!" I froze but the sheep smelled or saw us and headed west out of the basin. Carl stopped me from shooting at the running sheep, even though my target was in the lead. Guides are normally even tempered, but he was furious. We had stalked all day and had the sheep in our grasp. My screw-up of not having my gun within reach proved to be a costly one.

We proceeded to the top of the mountain, to the beautiful basin stretching north to where Bill and Jack had gone. We could see Bill and his guide through the scope half way up the slope. Their movements indicated they must be on a stalk. We saw many Stone rams on small outcroppings in their area. Carl, angry about blowing the stalk, decided to give up our altitude and return to camp.

My disappointment weighed heavily on the walk down. We picked up the horses and headed back to camp, less than a mile away. The cook and wrangler had the camp in order. They had firewood cut, split, and stacked. The aroma of fresh baked bread greeted us. Carl's anger was fanned by his knowledge that at this altitude the nice weather wouldn't last long. If it got foggy we wouldn't be able to get to the top of the mountains.

Joe and Bill returned sheepless. Bill had passed on a very respectable but badly broomed ram. His decision would turn out to be costly.

In retrospect, I learned sometimes; the first few days in an area are the best. We were the first hunters in the area for sheep this year. The animals had over a year without disturbance before we arrived. It became obvious that moving the camp would be difficult. But my spirits were still high. This was only the third day of the hunt.

The next day we got up early and hit the trail. I learned another trick to keep from getting saddle sore. If you walk the first fifteen or twenty minutes not only do you warm up, but you get rid of some of the previous day's soreness. We mounted the horses and made our way to the continental divide. I saw a beautiful six point bull elk and two good moose. Carl told me only one or two hunters a year made it to this spot because it was so far from main camp. We were about thirty miles due west and on the border of Gary's area.

About noon a rain squall hit. We sat under a small bush for shelter as there were no trees at this altitude. After the squall we checked the basins and walked over to Peck's area—home of Tushodi Lake rams. We spotted a total of thirty four ewes and lambs, but no rams.

An uneventful trip brought us back to camp and a hot home cooked meal. That night during the campfire conversations, we learned that most of Gary's help came from Hudson Hope or the Fort St. John area. The economy depended mainly on farming. The children all wanted to become guides since it provided a better source of income. We planned for the next day's hunt and headed for the sleeping bags. Since no one had been lucky, we decided to try some different areas.

The next day Carl opted to take Loren, the horse wrangler to give him more experience. We stopped a basin short of the divide. As we started across a rock scree, I twisted my ankle and fell. Pain shot through my leg, but I knew it wasn't broken. I wrapped it with an ace bandage from my day pack. Then I checked my gun which had hit hard. I had cracked the pistol grip on my Weatherby, but I hoped it hadn't knocked the scope out of alignment. I soon found out. Keeping up with Carl every day had taken it's toll.

We crossed the rock scree and made our way to the top of the mountain. A narrow point lead out to a ridge where we could glass another basin. We had lunch and rested. Carl went out on a very narrow point to set up the spotting scope. Twenty minutes later he waved for me and I slowly made my way out to the narrow point. I spotted a ram as he disappeared into a small gully. Carl told me eight rams had watered out of a small stream in the same gully.

We couldn't see them, so he wanted to go down. I panicked at the seventy degree slope. I was sure I would fall with my twisted ankle. A small game trail led over what looked like a load of gravel from the narrow point to the corner of the basin. I didn't think it would hold, but to my surprise it only gave slightly under foot. The noise we made was drowned our by the rushing of the stream. We made it to the stream head and crossed. Once over we slowly made our way down to a point Carl thought would be directly across from where the rams would reappear. Sure enough they came out of the stream bed and headed toward the edge of the valley floor. When all eight rams had emerged, we chose the largest.

We had a seat directly across from the rams. Using my knee for a rest I placed the cross hairs behind the shoulder and squeezed. The Weatherby literally bowled him over. He didn't move. The rams didn't want to leave their fallen comrade. This loyalty really surprised me. Finally a new leader headed out of sight taking the band with him.

We crossed the stream and headed for our trophy. The dark gray and black mixed with white made a beautiful cape. His horns measured thirty seven and one-half around the outside. We took pictures and found the bullet placement where it was supposed to be. Fortunately, my gun hadn't been knocked off by the fall.

We caped and quartered the animal. Loren got to carry out his first Stone ram. It didn't dawn on me until they left to get the horses that I had just completed half of my grand slam!

Stone sheep range between southern Yukon and northern British Columbia. They are slightly larger than Dall sheep with a big ram weighing in at over two hundred pounds. The rams stand thirty six inches at the shoulder and measures six feet in length. They vary in color from extremely light to nearly black.

The dark gray and black mixed with white made a beautiful cape. His horns measured thirty seven and one-half around the outside.

A Stone ram's horns curl more tightly than the Dall but are still thin. After what felt like an eternity, Carl and Loren returned. We loaded in the dark and headed for camp. The ride at night under the stars allowed me to quietly celebrate. Bill and Jack were more excited than I was to see our first ram. Carl worked on the cape while the cook fixed fresh ram loins. The meat tasted fantastic to me. We relived the stalk and kill many times before we headed for the sack.

My ankle had swollen during the night and Carl was still working with the skull, so we decided to take the day off. Carl, Loren, the cook, and I cleaned up around camp and split more wood for the stove.

We measured the ram and counted growth rings. He was ten years old and thirty seven and one half inches on each side with no brooming.

Jack returned in the middle of the day very excited with a broomed older ram. It didn't have the lamb tips he was looking for but was a true trophy. He and his guide shard the story of their tough trip across a sheer cliff to get into position above the lone ram on a ledge. Bill arrived later. He had seen nothing bigger than the previous ram he had taken.

Loren decided to stay in camp the next day. Carl and I headed back toward a small crossing where bear had forded the stream to head for a nearby berry patch. In the steepest part of the rock slides we spotted a mule deer buck high under a ledge. We climbed to a spot where we could see both drainages of Gathto Creek and glassed. We had lunch and watched some more. Memories of the previous year with Ray looking for the elusive grizzly drifted back. The sun began to set and we decided to head back to camp. Jack returned with a large Canadian moose. Caping and moving the meat had worn him out. Bill returned not having seen much. Carl decided to take the pack string back to base camp to get supplies and try a new area.

Up early the next day we packed and headed back to base camp. Riding behind the pack string with two ram skulls and a moose rack tied on the top was quite impressive. By late afternoon we arrived at camp, unpacked, and took much needed showers. We rehashed our stalks and kills with Gary.

The rams we had taken pleased him. Bill and his guide, Brian, had taken the long way home to no avail.

Gary thought we should rest a day while he took Bill to a little spot where rams might hide this time of year. Next day they were gone before breakfast. Four new elk hunters arrived at camp. Two of them were women hunters who had killed six point bulls. We spent the day packing for a camp toward the south of Gary's area. A herd of Rocky Mountain goats frequented a lick in the area. Bill and Jack both wanted to get a chance at one.

Bill and Gary returned about five. They had seen a group of six rams the largest of which would only go thirty six. Bill passed again. He was determined to get a forty-incher.

In the morning we packed up without the cook, and were off early. We headed down Gathto Creek, as I had done two years before, and headed south into the mountains. A long narrow trail led us over a large mountain. As we topped out a beautiful sight opened before us. Blue Lake was a large, spectacular lake situated on Gary's southern border. There were three cabins for fishing trips in the summer. We passed them about noon and continued east along a wide valley to the next range of mountains. We turned south again at the moose pasture where Tom and Tom, Jr., and Royal had killed their moose two years before. No moose were about, but we spotted a herd of caribou with a large bull. Too bad—the season wouldn't be open until next year.

It was almost dark by now so we made camp. Without the cook the meals were not nearly so inviting and the guides obviously didn't like doing the dishes. Next morning Bill and Jack headed for the lick. Carl and I went to the southern border of Gary's area. Here I got my first look at the drainage where L. S. Chadwick had killed what might be North America's most outstanding trophy. Gary Vince of Muskwa Safaris ran the premier Stone sheep area. The immenseness of this drainage was awesome. Turning back to where we had spotted some bear droppings close to a berry patch, we hid down wind and waited for a bear to approach.

It got late and we decided to head back for camp. Bill and Jack returned with grins on their faces and I knew they had both been successful. They had climbed a knife-like ridge and each found a billy on either side—without knowing the other was there. The guides busied themselves skinning and cleaning the skulls while Carl and I made dinner. Next day we packed and headed for the cabins at Blue Lake. We arrived in a heavy drizzle and found the shelter of the cabins and the beds welcome. We all celebrated and scheduled the next two days.

Carl and I planned to hike around the lake looking for bear. There was a recent black bear kill in the area and we were going to check it out. Jack would rest and Bill wanted to look for sheep.

Carl showed me the next day how Gary managed the area with controlled burns in the spring. The areas were full of browse for the animals. We didn't see a bear but got another look at the Muskwa drainage and managed to get soaking wet. Bill hadn't seen anything because of the rain and fog. He was disappointed since he only had one day left to hunt. Next day he would look for sheep while the rest of us took all the gear back to the main camp.

The following morning we retraced our path down the steep trail to Gathto Creek and back to base camp. We unpacked the horses and set about getting ready to leave the next day. While in camp I read a copy of *Safari Magazine*. I was amazed to discover this big game organization (Safari Club International) was dedicated to conservation and education. I talked to Gary about it. He told me he had twenty inner city youth last summer before hunting season. They all had a wonderful time. I couldn't imagine being exposed to such a beautiful area while still in my childhood. The stories of youngsters fishing and riding horses were just what I needed to convince me to join.

Bill returned after dark to tell us about spotting two rams, one of which was close to forty inches. They worked all day to get into position, then at the last moment the rams vanished over the ridge. Bill would go home without a ram, but with the satisfaction he had given it his all. The Texas physician (Peyton) returned with a heavy thirty eight inch ram on one side but broomed off about six inches from the base of the skull on the other side. Chester shot a respectable thirty six inch animal. They also took two bull moose and a black bear.

That night we celebrated with the guides over a wonderful meal and a few drinks. We learned the guides really appreciated hunters who could walk and shoot. This made us all feel good as we headed to bed. Once again Big Nine Outfitters proved this magnificent land in northern B.C. could produce some tremendous trophies.

We said our goodbyes and headed for Fort Nelson. Following a night's layover we headed back to Edmonton and home.

I met Gary the next year at Safari Club International's Convention in Las Vegas. He became a good friend and I was on his reference list from that time forward. The 1983 SCI convention honored Gary as the outstanding professional hunter of the year. Sadly, two years later he was killed trying to land in the fog at Fort Nelson. For North American big game hunting his death was a tragedy.

4

Spring Black Bear

After three successful fall hunts north to British Columbia and the Northwest Territories, I decided to try a spring hunt for black bear and grizzly in southern British Columbia. My quest lasted from the spring of 1980 until 1988.

A friend of mine who had hunted moose the previous fall with Len Pickering of Prince George, British Columbia, told me there was a good population of blacks and grizzlies in his area. I contacted Len and we set up a hunt for May 1980. Don Sillivan, a local real estate agent and avid hunter, was to accompany me.

We spent the first day on Flight 76 of Western Airlines from Denver to Edmonton. Edmonton, the crown jewel of Alberta, was as pretty as I had remembered it from the fall. Early the next morning we boarded Flight 41 which went from Edmonton to Grand Prairie and on to Ft. St. John, before terminating in Prince George. Prince George was much larger than the previous cities I had seen British Columbia. It had a population of some 90,000 people. We met Len Pickering, our guide and outfitter. After a brief shopping spree, we made the 2½ hour drive north and east to his base lodge and hunting area in the Anzac and Table River watersheds of the Rocky Mountains. His base is an old logging camp with all the comforts of home including four cabins heated with sheep-herder stoves, a gener-

Len Pickering, Bear Guide

ator supplies electricity, and separate bath houses with hot and cold running water.

We met Ken and Greg, Len's sons, who would be helping guide us for the next two weeks. We also met Murray who was in charge of the young guides. We saw flock after flock of waterfowl, a large cow moose, and a porcupine while driving to Len's guide area. Since it was my first spring trip to the north, the amount of waterfowl compared to the fall was amazing. The camp served meals family style and there was always plenty to eat. The talk around the table centered on bear hunting. The trip tomorrow would take us to a second camp about 12 miles away. From there we would hunt up into the mountains—backpacking where we could stay in mountain tents close to the game.

Ken and Murray would take Don and I and four pack horses to the next camp. The bears came come down initially in late March and early April, the warm weather in British Columbia this spring had caused them to go back up to find some comfort next to the snow banks.

A large six foot black bear skin graces the wall of Len's main camp. It was killed in the kitchen a few years back. His wife had been cleaning a large Dolly Varden caught in a nearby lake. Pictures on the wall displayed the quality of trophy grizzlies taken. They ranged between seven and nine feet in length.

We spent the next morning on horseback on a 12 mile pack trip starting at 7 and ending about noon at the upper camp. Mud slides were greening the shoots along the sides of the mountain. When we got to the upper camp we noticed a 7-8 inch paw print and claw marks above the door. The cabin had been built the year before with multiple spikes placed throughout to keep the bears from breaking in. However, they had managed to rip a corner of the camp apart and remove most of the food. After making camp, we hiked back to a meadow we had crossed which seemed like a likely spot bears would cross coming off the mountain. The weather was overcast.

We awoke the next morning with renewed vigor and started our hike up an 8500 foot mountain. We crossed snow fields to reach an area to set up our tent. The snow on the top was slight but enough to wet the slide areas to allow the green shoots to come up. On top was a beautiful crystal lake still half frozen. We made camp next to it. An A frame on top had fallen down from the battering of many years of storms. We set up camp and used part of the A-frame as a lean-to. We built a fire under it. That made it quite comfortable.

After lunch we headed for the slopes where we figured bears would be feeding. It was overcast and fog started to roll in. After glassing meadows for 2-3 hours we decided to head back to camp. We got to camp just as a storm blew in. After a quick dinner we crawled into our sleeping bags and raised the tent up as much as we could. The flapping sound of the wind was very strong. No one got much sleep.

The next morning found a few inches of new snow and a very strong front coming from the north east. This is an unusual pattern here since the weather usually comes from the Pacific. Following an excellent breakfast behind the lean to shelter, we decided it was probably fruitless to stay on top of the mountain in weather like this. So we packed up and headed down the six mile stretch back to the lower camp. At the second camp we fired the stove and the cook made a hearty dinner for all.

The trip down the mountain took nearly 10 hours less than the trip up and was a lot easier on everyone's shoulders and back. Green shoots appeared from 2000 feet off the mountain all the way to the base camp. This would provide the grizzly and black bears plenty of feed. It would probably make hunting very difficult. We glassed areas that night without seeing any bears, then headed back to camp.

That evening we heard scratching sounds and growling on the hill about 100 yards from camp. Don and Ken had seen a large black bear print and a sizeable grizzly track in the area. The smell of dinner had probably attracted a black bear. With guns ready, we stood watch at the camp door. The sounds got a little closer, but we never saw the bear.

The weather remained overcast, so we decided to move back to the main camp. Then we could use a four wheel drive to cover more ground. Don decided to do some fishing. Murray and I opted to ride up Table Road to Table Mesa which reportedly had a good black bear population. The road was bumpy and the last 4-5 days of rain had left many puddles and

We packed the horses and were back
to the main camp before the day was out.

deep potholes. We crossed the Anzac River and Parsnip and headed up Table Road. After driving 6-7 miles we parked at a small rock quarry. We walked up an old logging road to a small ridge. Murray and I split up so I could watch one ridge and he could keep an eye on the road at a cut slash area. Our signal was supposed to be a whistle if either saw any movement.

In about 30 minutes I heard a small whistle and Murray motioned me toward him. He was about 75 yards away. Hurrying to his stand, I looked down toward the road. We could see a large black bear moving toward the road. We got everything together and made our way back down the road. After we picked up his track, we stayed off the road and up above on a small ridge that faced the back side of the canyon. After running approximately another half mile I looked to the right and saw the bear grazing in a field 250 yards across the canyon. I was breathing heavily and was in no condition to make a good shot.

I took my hat and binoculars off and rested for a few seconds. I rested my gun on a small branch that was sticking out. The black bear moved continuously in a small field across the canyon. I took careful aim squeezed off a round. The black turned and ran 25 yards to the right, then circled around to the back. My next shot stood him straight up, but he took off toward the mountain top. We waited about half an hour before we crossed to where the bear had been. We found very little blood around the site where he had been feeding. Our disappointment was acute as we checked the surrounding areas and again found very little blood.

The black had torn up some trees in his path to the top of the mesa. Following him we made our way to the top and broke into a clearing. We could still only see 25 or 30 yards in any direction. We made our way slowly down a small overgrown logging road. Then we heard a menacing growl and timber break as the bear scurried away in front of us. We made our way through the scrub alders and slash timber to a small pine tree he had crawled over and broken many branches. We approached the next ravine as the bear let out a ferocious bawl. We felt we were very close.

We searched the wash and found the bear leaning against a tree on the other side of the ravine. He was obviously badly hurt. I crawled to where I could find a steady rest and fired one shot. The bear crumbled in a ball and rolled down to the bottom of the basin where he breathed his last gasp. As we approached we noticed he was much larger than we had first thought. Murray calculated his weight to be right at 325-350 pounds. He measured 7 feet 6 inches.

The first shot was at 7 o'clock but by the time we got to the bear it was 8:30. Darkness was quickly approaching. We worked furiously to skin and cape him before dark. Fortunately, the weather is pleasant this time of year and it stays relatively light until nearly 10 o'clock. This allowed us to make our way back to the truck before darkness enveloped us. I took both guns and binoculars while Murray carried the cape back to the truck. Approaching Table Road we saw another black bear on the side of the road. Murray went after the truck while I washed my hands, face, and took a long needed drink of icy water. Murray was soon back with the truck. We put the hide and cape in the back, and slowly headed for to camp. It was close to midnight when we got in. All the lights out.

The bear had thick black hair with no rub spots, a good bear for a mild spring.

But everyone was soon awake and welcomed us with a warm meal and hearty congratulations. Don and Kenny had gone fishing and caught an 8 pound Dolly Varden and several large Arctic char. While fishing they saw a hefty black bear in the tree and they found some small cub tracks in the area. So they backed off and left the bear in the tree. After retelling my bear chase, we decided to head for bed.

The next morning Murray finished caping the bear. A strong morning wind blew in clouds. It started to rain furiously. Since we were unable to make any type of stalk today, we cleaned the bear hide and the camp. At noon Len returned with two hunters who had been at the lake cabin for five days. They had caught some 8 pound Dolly Varden and had some excellent fishing. However they had only seen one black bear. Vic, an avid bow hunter, had gotten within 50 yards when the bear smelled them and headed for cover. Although there were three carcasses around the lake cabin, no black bears were feeding on them. Smitty and Vic had experienced our same problem with almost constant rain. After swapping stories of the last five days' hunts, we settled down to a scrumptious meal of Dolly Varden steak and moose meat. This, combined with Northern HP sauce and homemade bread, was all we needed. We settled down for the long night.

We hoped the next day to be able to put on a long stalk. The next morning we headed for our previous bear kill. We drug it into an open spot where it could be seen and covered it with smelly material and fish entrails. The rest of the day we spent on Table Road and Reynolds Creek looking at the slashes and other forms of wildlife and waterfowl. Walking along the road we heard voices coming from the woods. It was Don and Kenny. They had just shot a 6½ foot cinnamon bear. It was a beautiful brown-coated boar. We helped them carry it to the truck. After we got them off for camp, we spent the rest of the time walking the road checking the slashes on the green hills for any grizzly coming out in the late afternoon. The warm weather and the rain had caused the hills to turn lush green and had thickened the underbrush to where it was hard to walk through.

We spent the next few days taking pictures of waterfowl, moose, porcupine, beaver, scouting the Anzac River, and following Reynolds Creek up to the railroad bridge where we had planted the carcass. We saw fresh footprints in the muddy grounds surrounding the area but were unable to pick up a fresh grizzly track. We followed some of the logging roads up into a fresh cut that was to be replanted that summer. Still no grizzly. Grizzly tracks are easy to spot compared to black bear prints. They are much larger and sport a claw mark at the end of each toe. Even after seeing many sets of tracks we were unable to spot a bear.

That afternoon we set out for Prince George to get our black bear export permits. We had minimal difficulty with the British Columbia Fish and Game Service. We returned with export permits in hand. As we rode up Table Road one more time we saw an extra large grizzly track. Still no sight of bear though. That night Sherry, Len's daughter, returned from Williams Lake. She said they were having trouble finding black or grizzly bears due to the rain and the warm spring. The camp she worked had taken one grizzly. But they had seen nothing for the last three weeks.

Hunting wasn't getting better, so we packed and readied ourselves for the trip back to Denver. The terrain in southern British Columbia differed greatly from the north. The mountains were less steep and not very high. The rivers were wider and the dense cover surrounding the banks made vision difficult. This heavy cover made it great bear country. It also offered the predators of the moose, elk, and caribou an advantage. It's easy to wee why this kept their population much lower than in northern British Columbia.

The flight from Prince George back to Denver was long but allowed us to reflect on the 9-10 inch grizzly tracks we followed more than once into the thick brush. It also gave us a fresh awakening observing all the waterfowl mating and nesting in the spring. Seeing and photographing some unusual duck pairs only added to this first spring hunt.

5

Alaska –
The First Trip

My father wanted to find a hunt where he could take a moose and caribou. I decided if I could arrange a hunt on the Alaskan Peninsula for both species I'd accompany him. The weather there was usually mild and I needed the Alaska-Yukon moose and the Barren Ground caribou for my collection. The walking wouldn't be too tough, which was good since my dad was sixty-two.

I wrote a lot of letters before choosing Gary LaRose of Palmer, Alaska. We exchanged correspondence about times, gear, and flights. The hunt would take place the first ten days of October because that was the only time when both species could be taken. I made the arrangements and September was soon upon us.

Dad and I met in Seattle and went on to Alaska. We were in Anchorage before we realized it since we were busy catching up on our home state hunting trips. Upon arrival we checked our bags and marveled at the full mounts of Alaskan Game in the Anchorage airport terminal.

We laid over in Anchorage and headed out the next morning for King Salmon. We met a few other hunters waiting for the plane in Anchorage. I was happy to learn Tom Phillippe,

Jr. and his dad were also flying to King Salmon to go on a self guided caribou hunt. On the plane we discussed the events of the past three years. Tom, Jr. was now the president of the nursing home chain. His dad was the chairman of the board. He had gotten a Dall and Stone sheep, along with some other species, since our last meeting.

We vowed to meet at the next Foundation of North American Sheep Convention and continued to discuss hunting. This chance meeting joined me with one of my closest hunting companions. Over the next few years we would spend a lot of nights under the stars together.

King Salmon and Dillingham are the jumping off points for the peninsula. After saying goodbye to Tom and Tom, Jr., we bought our hunting and fishing licenses. Peninsula Airways was our waiting point for Gary at the airport. He showed up carrying four large, fresh king crab, indicating we would have them for dinner. We loaded our gear in the 210 and headed south toward Pumice Creek. We passed Pilot Point and Ugashik before descending into Gary's camp. Landing on the cinder tracks was a new experience but would soon become old hat as we used this for most of our travels while here.

We got situated in a very comfortable quonset hut
with an oil stove for heat.

Two other hunters were in camp, one from Texas and one from Pennsylvania.

After we unpacked our gear, Gary flew us to a river not far away. He landed on a gravel bar so we could get some fishing in before the hunt. The supercub, the backbone of the Alaskan bush pilot, had amazing maneuverability and ability to land and take off on short distances. The balloon tires they used for the gravel bars and tundra allowed them to land and take off almost anywhere. We caught eight to twelve pound salmon on almost every cast. The fishing license only allowed us to keep two fish. My dad thought he had died and gone to heaven. My arms were getting sore by the time Gary came back and we headed for camp and a supper of king crab. He explained that the major portion of the caribou migration had passed but they were still seeing good caribou every day. The ones on the peninsula migrated west and north coming out of the mountains as they headed for King Salmon.

Dad thought he had died and gone to heaven.

Over a hearty breakfast Gary explained he was a guide short until his son arrived. He would fly my dad and I down to the same stream we fished on at the spike camp to look for caribou until Gary, Jr. arrived. We met our guide, Sam, who would be my dad's guide throughout the hunt and headed south. Soon we set up camp and started spotting caribou. Unable to fly and hunt on the same day, we made dinner early and headed for the sleeping bag. That night it had rained and froze and the hot morning coffee sure tasted good over breakfast. We walked the cinder tracks between the bogs and kept glassing for caribou. We got to a place where we could see the Bering Sea and the large flat plain between. We set up the spotting scope but saw nothing but small bulls during the day.

I learned a very tough lesson on the way back to camp. Just as we came over a rise, I spotted a trophy caribou about three hundred yards out in the bog. He turned tail as soon as he spotted us. By the time I was steady enough to shoot he was out of range. I thought since he had to round a corner that I could cut across the cinder track and head him off. Much to my dismay, after I made the cut (about a mile and fifteen minutes later) he was still about two miles ahead. Slowly I made it back to camp and dinner. Next morning over breakfast we heard Gary's plane coming. He picked me up and took me back to base camp to meet his son.

I then met Charlie who had taken a strange fifty five inch moose. One side was twisted in an odd fashion probably due to an injury to the antler in early growth. Charlie Barnhill had taken a month off from the oil boom in Texas to hunt moose, caribou, and bear. He was flying to Gary's Kodiak Island Camp after this hunt to hunt for brown bear. We met briefly and soon found out we had a lot of hunting in common. Over the years I visited a few of his oil properties for some great whitetail deer and quail hunting. We rushed a little to get ready to fly to the east side of the peninsula to try for a big moose. Gary's son loved to fly and had built his plane. He had brought another enthusiast with him. Garland was a north slope engineer on holiday and would come in handy if we downed a moose.

After loading Gary, Jr.'s newly rebuilt 206 we headed north on the peninsula then east to Wide Bay. We crossed an area close to where active volcanos were smoking and soon spotted the bay. Descending we saw some nice moose in this basin and hoped they would stick around till morning. Landing on the beach was quite a trick since the driftwood had not been cleaned to make a runway. Luckily the tide was out and we finally found a spot to set down. The tents were up in short order. We decided to hit the sack so we could get an early start in the morning. I heard a lot of war stories from these two young pioneers of our northern most state before I fell asleep.

I could hear the wind blowing when I woke up, but was ill prepared for coming events. After a brief breakfast we headed out to look for the moose we'd had spotted the day before. Walking up a shallow creek bed to get to higher ground, we heard a moose grunt but never did see him. We decided the only advantage would be to get as high as possible. We climbed onto a rocky ledge underneath a glacier, spent as long as we could in the cold wind, then decided to head for the tents. The slow drizzle soon turned into a downpour. The wind was much worse at the camp and we noticed one of the tents looked kind of funny. The tide was in. We now had to ford the small slough we had stepped over on the way out. One tent had blown on top of the other. We re-anchored the tents. I crawled into one and Garland into the other. Worried about his plane, Gary, Jr. went to check it. For two days he returned only for meals.

The storm came in and stayed. It was brutal. We were afraid to leave the tents for fear they would blow away. We got together for meals we cooked in Garland's tent, then returned to our own dens to wait it out. I had the only reading material. I would read 100 pages of the novel, tear them out, and hand them to Garland. For two days and two nights the wind and rain was relentless. It's one of the few times I've run out of something to read. Garland and I became very good friends talking about how he got to Alaska and how much he enjoyed the outdoors.

Finally on the third morning we woke to bright light from the sun coming up on the east side of the peninsula. Before we started breakfast we noticed something strange on top of the water. At first we thought it was a pack of wolves running on the beach. Then we determined it was antlers sticking out of the water. Your eyes will play tricks on you after being in the dark for so long. It was a herd of caribou swimming the bay, their antlers glimmering in the sunrise behind them. I hurried to put my clothes on but made a serious error of not grabbing a hat or jacket.

Soon I was soaked from the waist down because the two day rain left everything wet. Gary and I ran to where we thought the caribou would come out of the water. They love to walk on creek beds and we thought they would head for this area to get to higher ground. We settled down behind some alders and sure enough the caribou came out of the water and headed up the creek bed. We were about seventy five yards from them and studied them closely. Most were cows and small bulls. Then we noticed a tremendous bull coming out of the water with long tines and very good bez and shovels. I had read a lot about judging a caribou and the main rule is to start from the top down. This caribou had everything! Suddenly I realized how cold and wet I was. I managed to get my gun loaded and steadied it against the alder bush. The bull was walking in the midst of the small bulls and cows. Finally he stepped clear and I put the cross hairs on the front shoulder. He fell as the gun roared.

We walked over to the caribou and marveled at the long
tines—measuring over twenty four inches.

Gary and I caught movement behind the caribou and suddenly knew why they were moving. An eight to nine foot brown bear was on the beach heading our way. The echo of the shot must have scared him, because he changed directions in a hurry.

After taking pictures we caped and quartered the caribou and carried it to the plane. Gary had taken a smaller bull for the freezer. Here his skills as a Safeway meat cutter came in handy. We had no way of knowing what the weather was going to do so we finished our breakfast and decided to go back to base camp. We cleared a runway on the beach and took off for the west side of the peninsula. None of the moose we had seen before were in the basin as we left. The weather must have moved them. A short ride over the pass and we headed south to Ugashik and base camp.

I was quite weary from the time spent in my tent trying to avoid the wind and rain. I took a leisurely sponge bath and a long walk to stretch my legs. It was great to return to a camp that was warm and to have dry clothes. The cinders in the area made the walking easy but Gary told me to be back by early afternoon. There were only two hunting days left and we were to fly to another area for moose that afternoon. I learned my dad had taken a good caribou and was hunting for moose at another spike camp. Charlie had finished his hunt and was ready for the trip to Kodiak for bear. He was relaxed and eager for the rigors of the thick alders on Kodiak. Later I found out he took a nice ten foot brown bear but got weathered in for five days in a small cabin. By the time the plane came to get him he was about to walk out. The meat was racked and the cape fleshed and salted.

We flew over to see how my dad was doing. We noticed he and Sam were in the middle of a moose stalk. The moose in this area had to be over fifty inches and this one sure qualified. We did not want to spook it so we flew off to a high plateau covered with cinders. Gary landed and we unloaded the gear for a spike camp similar to what we had on the east side of the peninsula. Since Gary needed the cub to land in this area, I waited while he went to get Gary, Jr. Soon they returned and the three of us set up camp. We were on the edge of a huge drainage that was about a half mile across and as long as the eye could see. The valley ran from the Pacific side to where it met Wide Bay in the east. We worked our way over the edge of the ridge and sat down to glass. We both spotted the large white horns in the afternoon sun.

We kept looking and found two more. We judged all to be above the fifty inch limit. We wondered if they would be there in the morning. We made our way back to camp and made dinner. It never ceases to amaze me how the simplest of food tastes wonderful after a long day of walking and hunting. We talked a lot about the stalk planned for the morning if the moose remained in the basin. And about how handy Gary, Jr.'s meat cutting experience came in on these hunts. He certainly had taken the caribou apart deftly. He said a moose was a lot harder to cut up since it was about three times the size of a caribou.

The sunset was beautiful from our vantage point. We crawled into the sleeping bag with thoughts of moose on our minds. It sure felt good to be in dry clothes and have a warm meal before starting what was sure to be a long day.

Gary, Jr. had coffee boiling as soon as I got dressed. We knew we would have to move quickly and quietly so we packed light. I carried my gun and one knife while Gary took a day pack with lunches and knives. Even though we were sheltered from the valley to the north, we tried not to make much noise. We made our way to the ridge again, where we sat down to glass. The sun was starting to light the valley floor and soon we spied our three moose. They hadn't moved much. While we watched, one headed north past the largest and on out of the valley over the far ridge. We hoped he hadn't spooked the other two. After what felt like an eternity we planned the route for the stalk.

We had to go about two hundred yards through alders to the valley floor. Then we would have to cross a small stream and make our way into range on the flat valley floor. Luckily the moose were feeding slowly up the side of the far ridge. They should be visible from the valley floor. The problem was, we could be seen as soon as we came onto the valley floor. We also worried about the sun warming the air and our scent rising toward the moose. Getting down the ridge was easy until we got to the valley floor. Here we encountered alders so thick we had to crawl through them to the stream. Waders made crossing the stream easy but the gravel bar had large bear tracks all over. There's always an eerie feeling when one finds a large bear track. The moisture conceals the age of the track, leaving some doubt in one's mind.

We picked our way through the alders and up to higher ground. Here they thinned out and we spotted the moose about two hundred and fifty yards away.

Gary whispered, "Get behind me and stay low."

We crept between, around, and through alder patches as though we were another moose for approximately a hundred yards. We were as close as we could get and had to shoot. There was no rest so Gary, Jr. knelt in front of me and I used his shoulder as a rest. I placed the cross hairs on the moose's shoulder and fired. It didn't even flinch, yet I thought I'd hit him solid. I fired twice more. Each time there was little to see. Gary told me not be worry because I had hit him solid three times. The big bull finally took one step up the hill and fell over.

Caping and taking the horns off a moose is a major undertaking. The horns alone weigh up to ninety pounds.

One cannot realize how an animal can stand with three well placed bullets from a modern high powered in it until you examine an Alaskan-Yukon moose. This largest of the deer family weighs between sixteen and eighteen hundred pounds, stands six and one-half feet high, and is ten and one-half feet long. His horn was stuck in the bushes and it took two of us to get it out enough to take pictures. After congratulations were offered the work began. In Alaska all the edible meat must be taken out of the field.

Quartering the animal, Gary's meat cutting ability again came into play. Every load was backbreaking and on the third I twisted my ankle rather bad. Waders are great for the water and bogs but provide little ankle support. With only Gary and I, getting all the meat, cape, and horns to where the plane could land was quite a job. We worked all day and into the evening getting it to a small landing strip about a quarter of a mile up the valley.

Finally in early evening Gary flew over and landed to help us get the meat. After several loads Gary, Jr. and I headed for the camp to tear it down. We had eaten all the food and the spike tent was down before Gary could get back to pick us up. Soon we saw the Cub circling to land. We loaded it full and crawled in with the horns tied on the struts of the airplane.

Gary said it was the heaviest he had been in this spot. He only had a short runway. The engine revved and soon we were down the cinder track and airborne. Before long the main camp quonset hut came into view.

When we landed, my dad was waiting on the runway. I learned they had taken the moose we had seen but another moose wouldn't leave it thinking it had been injured in a fight. They finally shot over the animal to get it to leave the area. He congratulated me on my trophy before he noticed I was limping severely. After exchanging tales of our moose hunt, we had a wonderful dinner. Stories echoed long into the night. Charlie was gone but the hunter from Pennsylvania had returned. He spent three days in a small cabin with his guide waiting out the storm—only to find all the moose had left. He returned to take a wide, heavy beamed caribou but it had very short tines that looked like runners on a sled.

A few bear had been spotted but none of any significant size and proximity to make them worrisome. Bear hunting on the peninsula took place every other year and this was the off

Dad with his trophy

year. Gary said the bears sensed it and were always more aggressive toward the hunter and their camps in the off years. My ankle was extremely sore and I had trouble going to sleep that night. But the satisfaction of my two animals and the fact my dad had taken two animals made sleep a little easier.

After breakfast the next morning we loaded the plane and headed for King Salmon. We said our goodbyes to Gary and Gary, Jr., then waited for the jet to Anchorage. Gary promised to take the horns to D&C Expediters who would flesh and dry the capes before shipping them with the horns.

When I landed in Anchorage I could hardly walk. We stayed overnight at the Sheraton-Anchorage with my foot elevated and packed in ice. The Next day we flew to Seattle where my dad went to Pittsburgh and I headed for Glenwood Springs. On my return I found out Tom, Tom, Jr., and their party had taken four Boone and Crockett caribou just north of us.

My first trip to Alaska assured my return. The country is immense and the terrain varied. The peninsula with its actual volcanos and cinder tracks, streams full of salmon, and flats full of caribou allowed a closer look as only one of these varying terrains.

Dad after ten days on the Alaskan Peninsula.

6

Colorado Hunting

With the successful trips to British Columbia and the Northwest Territories behind me, I started to look for species I could get closer to home. Western Colorado has a good population of mountain lion. After talking to many people I realized this could be done as an *on call hunt*. This meant I could work while the outfitter was trying to cut a track. The prime months for mountain lion are December through February while there is an abundance of fresh snow for tracking. A lion is tracked with dogs who tree or ledge it until the hunter can get within shooting distance.

This sounds easy but can be anything but. The high country in these months is often bitter cold with waist deep snow that makes travel almost impossible. The older Tom's are notorious for jumping from the tree and running. If the dogs can keep up, the lion will usually tree again a few miles away. When I asked about lions the name Chuck Griffin kept coming up. After hunting season we got together to discuss the possibility of a lion hunt. Cat hunters are a different breed, they have pickups with dog boxes on top. They have a second sense about the dogs they work and always seem to know what the dogs will do next. They know how much the dogs can take.

I made my deposit and went about my business of doctoring, hoping for a phone call with Chuck on the other end. Finally it came, Chuck said he had found a fresh track and that we should go in the morning. I rearranged my schedule and got ready. It was early December and snow had fallen heavily over the last few weeks. Later I learned that a good friend of Chuck's, Pete Sherwood, had cut the fresh track while trapping. Pete was from Eagle, Colorado, which meant the track had to be east of Glenwood Canyon.

The next morning I met Chuck at seven for breakfast. It was still dark. The M&M Cafe in Glenwood was a hang out for hunters and truckers. After a little local color, I climbed into Chuck's pickup for the ride to Gypsum. We picked up Pete and headed north out of town on a secondary road which climbed to the top of the first snow covered mesa. It ended in a turnaround, so we stopped and unloaded the snowmobile.

After letting fresh dogs loose we drove on the snowmobile for about two miles around to where Pete had cut the track. Sure enough there was a fresh scent and soon the dogs were baying and running ahead of us. The sound seemed to get further and further away. Then after a few miles it seemed to be getting closer. We stopped on a ridge and could see all the dogs at a base of a large pinon tree. In the highest branches was a mountain lion.

We started across the slope but soon the sound of the dogs got more distant. The lion was on the move again. The snow on the north slope was three to four feet deep and very powdery. It made walking very tough. The powder pants and Sorels kept me dry. I began to sweat with so many clothes on. Soon we were under the tree and Chuck told me the cat had spent the night in the previous tree. His clue was it had urinated a few times around the base. Chuck thought the animal must have a kill close by. He was sure it was a large tom.

We took off after the dogs. They were around the hill to the west about a half mile away. This time as we approached the tree the largest dog was in one of the lower branches and had the cat at bay. We took pictures and positioned ourselves for an open shot. I put a shot behind the front shoulder with my Ruger .22 magnum pistol. The cat's tail straightened and he slid out of the tree. The dogs immediately pounced on him but there was no fight.

After taking pictures and admiring this beautiful predator,
the work of getting him home started.

I wanted to mount him life-size so we didn't gut him. That way Chuck could skin him. We were about four miles from the truck (all uphill) with a hundred and forty pound mountain lion. What a struggle. The three to four feet of snow didn't make matters any easier. We decided to send Chuck back to the truck while Pete and I dragged the cat downhill toward the Colorado River. The first hundred yards was easy since it was straight down, but soon we were maneuvering down a narrow canyon and the dragging became harder. It was now late afternoon and the sun was down in the west. It was very cold in the shade.

Just as exhaustion was about to do me in we saw the river. After a short drag to a railroad bridge, we found Chuck waiting with the truck and a welcome hot cup of coffee. We headed for the check station and met the game warden to certify the kill. It was a happy trip back through the canyon to Glenwood. After showing the cat to the family and a few friends, Chuck took it to skin it. He left the pelt at the taxidermist. This ended one of the most pleasurable hunting trips I ever experienced.

The next year, after a successful Stone sheep hunt, I began looking for another species to go after. Buffalo hunting in the lower forty-eight has become limited to private ranches with huntable populations. Alan Baier of Little Creek Ranch in Colbran, Colorado was a well known outfitter for buffalo. I had met him a few times at the SCI convention. The fact that his ranch was only ninety miles away was quite convenient. National forest borders his ranch on two sides and the buffalo range free. This made the hunt more challenging. I set a date with Alan for late November. Deer and Elk season were over and he said the hair of the buffalo would be longer then.

I planned a long weekend and headed west toward Grand Junction. As I turned and headed up a long narrow canyon to Alan's house I couldn't help but wonder what this country must have been like in the days when only the Indians called these hills home.

Alan's hospitality was genuine and his beautiful log home was decorated with many trophies from past hunting trips. I would bunk in the basement then go to the ranch in the morning for the hunt.

Alan awoke me about six with a hot cup of coffee. After a hearty breakfast we were on our way. Little Creek Ranch was about twelve miles from Alan's home. Soon we pulled into the farm house where my guide, Les Severson, met us. After introductions we decided to head out on a scouting trip. There were six inches of fresh snow. "It should be easy to spot and track the animals if we cross their sign," said Les.

We headed up the closest ridge and soon could see almost to Colbran, which was seven miles away. The day was bright but cold as we glassed for grazing animals. We hoped to spot them from a good distance, then stalk them much like sheep. The snow was quiet so our stalk should go quite well as long as we stayed downwind of the animals. Topping the rise we saw a beautiful four point mule deer out browsing. He acted as if he knew the season had ended two weeks before. We rode a circular route back to the ranch house for lunch but didn't see any sign of buffalo. With this much land to roam I wondered if I had enough time.

Lunch consisted of hot soup and sandwiches which hit the spot. Alan said after a storm like we had just experienced the buffalo tended to head for the thick scrub oak for protection from the wind and snow. That afternoon we headed for the northeast corner of the ranch where the cover was the thickest. After about an hour ride we perched on a windy point looking east toward the national forest. Les became excited. He saw some movement in the scrub oak at the very corner of the ranch. After much help from Les, I finally spotted the same brown movement. We saw three large bulls grazing at the edge of the scrub oaks. We knew we would have to be quiet—and lucky—to get a shot before they disappeared into the cover.

We rode to a point about a half mile above and upwind from the buffalo. We tied the horses and started down slope in knee deep snow. We kept the largest buffalo in sight until we entered the scrub oak. For the next half hour we walked slowly and crawled uncomfortably through the scrub to try to get close to the buffalo. Snow kept falling down the back of my neck from the overhanging branches. I was getting colder by the minute. Finally Les, a few yards in front of me, motioned me to stop.

I couldn't see anything but snow. Then he signaled me forward. We crept a few more feet but kept well hidden in the scrub oak. Across a small meadow a large brown bull slowly ambled out of the scrub oak. He was feeding but looked up every few seconds to check his surroundings. He never ventured more than two steps from the scrub oak. I was sure he was going to disappear any minute. Les whispered, "I don't think he will come out any further so you need to shoot from here." I put my gun up after removing the scope cover—and could only see snow.

Finally after moving slightly, I found an opening where I could see the top of his shoulder. The buffalo was feeding left to right as I put the cross hairs behind the shoulder and squeezed. The gun fired but the buffalo didn't move. I reloaded and fired again. Still no movement. At Les's insistence, I reloaded and fired again. "You hit him good—I saw the dust fly," Les exclaimed. The bull started to run as I fired my last round. He still managed to make it fifty yards through the scrub oak before falling. Les was jumping up and down as I got to the bull. The animal was huge. It took three of us to roll him upright for a picture. I learned I'd hit him squarely all four times. I was impressed with the amount of lead this large animal could take.

After a lot of work we got the animal back to the ranch and skinned. We celebrated with a wonderful dinner at Alan's house and spent the evening telling stories around the fire. After breakfast the next morning I said goodbye and headed back to Glenwood Springs.

I kept thinking about what an experience it must have been for early western settlers to see thousands of these magnificent beasts roaming the plains.

The animal was huge.
It took three of us to roll him upright for a picture.

7

Rocky Mountain High

Before I can tell the story of my third sheep taken in Colorado high country, I need to explain the complexities of the permit system used in most states. Usually eighty percent of the permits for a certain species go to the residents of that state. This leaves very few permits for all the hunters from other states. The two of the hardest species to collect permits for are the Shiras moose and the Rocky Mountain bighorn. The *absolute* hardest is the desert bighorn with about fifteen nonresident permits for all the United States, except Arizona and Nevada. Since there are almost unlimited permits to anyone who can pay the fee in Mexico, it takes this species out of the drawing system. Being a resident of Colorado gave me the opportunity to apply in Colorado for this once in a lifetime permit. (Since then, the sheep herd has done so well and the kill ratio is so low due to the altitude and terrain— Colorado has made it an every five year permit). Colorado has also added Shiras moose and desert sheep permits to residents on an extremely limited basis.

Upon returning from a life long dream of a three week safari in Zambia, I found the resident permit for Rocky Mountain bighorn waiting. I had lucked out and drawn in S13E, which translates to area thirteen east. This consists of an area with some of the most beautiful scenery in the U.S.A.

From here we could see all Maroon Creek and the Conumdrum Valley.
Pyramid Peak and the Maroon Bells were readily visible
across the valley.

Sievers mountain was to the right and a favorite wintering ground of the bighorns in the area. Pyramid Peak, a majestic mountain, was to the south. The Snowmass-Maroon Bells wilderness area has four mountains over fourteen thousand feet and is some of the most scenic country in Colorado. Aspen borders the northern boundary of the area. I started looking for someone to help me in getting my sheep. A friend, Dale Paas, had taken a sheep three years before on East Maroon Creek. I heard of a local outfitter named Al Cluck who had successfully taken a sheep the previous year. After exchanging phone calls, we met to work out details of the hunt.

The season was from September 10 to October 1. I only wanted to hunt the weekends so as not to disrupt my work schedule, if at all possible. The area suited this type of hunting since four major drainages and three ridges in between made up ninety percent of the huntable terrain. The altitude was from eighty five hundred to thirteen thousand feet with most of the country above timberline. We had five weeks to scout and took full advantage of the situation. Another friend, Dave Force, is an accomplished mountain pilot. He had grown up on the western slope and had a good feel for flying in and around high mountain peaks. We decided to fly about once a week for the next five weeks to see if we could spot any sheep.

I was not ready for the excitement of flying in and around the ridges. The scenery was awesome from the air. We saw sheep every time we flew. We came to the conclusion that most ewes and lambs were on East Maroon Creek. The rams were on East Snowmass Creek. Al wanted the hunt to be strictly backpack and I agreed. This way we could move camps if we didn't see sheep or the weather became unreasonable. Al and Annie took the camp in a week before the season started and things were ready.

I had stayed in reasonably good shape and needed only to carry my gun and a twenty pound pack. The season opened on a Saturday, but we hiked in to Willow Lake on Thursday to acquaint ourselves with the terrain. Leaving the Maroon Bells parking lot at seven in the morning we hiked straight up three thousand feet before topping out on a small ridge above

Willow Lake. The camp sat on the northwest corner of the lake in a sheltered clump of scrub trees. Once down in the basin we could glass all the surrounding side hills to check for sheep. We took off our packs, made camp, and consumed a tasty lunch. Then I did a little trout fishing in Willow Lake and soon we knew what was for dinner. After dinner we set up the spotting scope and glassed the surrounding mountains for sheep. Not seeing any we cooked the trout and tested our sleeping bags.

Next morning there was dew on the ground and hot coffee tasted wonderful. Annie stayed in camp while Al and I hiked into some surrounding basins. Al showed me where he had taken his ram the year before and in the same small basin there was again fresh sign. Next we slipped over a small ridge to look into Waterfall Basin, a sizeable basin behind the Snowmass ski resort. There was a herd of about thirty elk grazing in the lush grass still available in the high alpine basins. We continued down Willow Creek to look into the next valley. This one was very steep; both sides were covered with rock scree.

Having no luck, we headed back to camp for a late lunch. We went to Buckskin Pass after lunch, where we saw twenty ewes and lambs. By the time we got back to camp we were dragging. Dinner was delicious and soon we settled into the sleeping bags for a well deserved rest.

Morning came with a surprise: four inches of snow. In September any kind of weather should be expected in the high alpine meadows. But still surprised us. The warm breakfast was welcome before we headed out for the first day. The storm had blown through and patches of blue were showing in the sky. We previously decided to hunt the ridge between main Snowmass and East Snowmass Creeks. This was a long ridge with basins on the west side where we had seen rams while flying. We climbed out of the basin and over Willow Pass into East Snowmass Creek drainage. Staying high on the west side we crossed one remaining snow field and soon were on the ridge line. The sun was very bright now and the snow was melting quickly. The first of three basins we looked in was empty except for melting snow. The second surprised us with four mule deer bucks carrying impressive antlers. It was mid morning and the wind had picked up but it was blowing in a direction that allowed us not to worry about anything we spotted in the basins.

The next basin was the one where we expected to find sheep. It had a small pool of melted snow at the top and rock pinnacles for easy escape on the north. As we peered over the top of the ridge we spotted four rams feeding about half way down and on the northern edge of the basin. We set up the spotting scope and discovered only one was legal. A legal ram in this area had to have a three quarter curl. The ram looked like he would go twenty eight to thirty two inches but we were still four to five hundred yards away. We could stalk but we would occasionally be in sight of the rams. They finally bedded down about noon with the largest ram on a small ledge.

We left Annie and our packs to see if we could get a closer look. She was to watch through the spotting scope and motion if the sheep moved. We headed down out of sight using the ridge as cover until we were at the small pool. Here we had to cross an area where there was no cover until we got into some steep rock ledges. Then we could cross the basin for a closer look.

We made it to the rocks and motioned to Annie, who relayed the sheep had not moved by way of a hand signal. As we started to cross the rocks I noticed the wind was blowing toward the sheep. We crept slowly to a predetermined point where we would be only about one hundred yards away. Looking over the top we should have been able to see the ram on the ledge. And there was no movement and no ram. We made our way across the basin and soon were standing on the ledge where the ram had bedded down. From here it was easy to see how their getaway was so easy. There were ledges and short cover everywhere. We crawled our way back out of the basin. We later learned from Annie that half way across—while we were still out of sight—the largest ram had stood up, looked our way, and simply walked off the ledge and out of sight.

We returned to camp quite disappointed. That night my sleeping bag never felt so good. Watching a clear Colorado sky at eleven thousand feet curled up in your sleeping bag is hard to describe. The stars look as though you can reach out and touch them.

Next morning Al decided we should investigate the lower portion of Willow Creek. That would allow us to watch Sievers Peak all day. We moved slowly around the first scree field and came to a small chute which one could climb over and look into Waterfall Basin. Topping the ridge we noticed two nice bucks off to our left climbing straight up and into East Snowmass Creek. Next we saw the largest mule deer I've ever seen trotting across the basin. He finally laid down under a small outcropping on the far side.

Al and Annie decided to climb the far ridge and check for fresh sheep sign. I set up the spotting scope and glassed Sievers Peak. I noticed a very nice six point bull herding his harem of cows directly across the valley. The wind was severe on the ridge and soon another small squall blew through making vision impossible. I waited until I could see Al cross the ridge and head back down before I started off the ridge. We met at the base of Willow Creek and wound our way back to camp, keeping Sievers Peak in view all the way. We barely got back as dark settled in; then we sat around the fire discussing the next day's plans. Al and I decided to cross over to East Snowmass Creek and walk to the trailhead. Annie would walk out the same way we had come in and take the car around to meet us.

The air was crisp as Annie made morning coffee and we were soon on our way over Willow Pass. We crossed the snowfield again and headed for the ridge. The first basin had a herd of elk that had gathered after the snow. The second one again contained the timberline bucks we had seen two days before. We made our way up to the edge of the third basin and peered over the edge. We glassed all reaches of the basin to no avail. After a few hours we decided to investigate the ridges where we'd seen the sheep. We made our way across the basin and found many places with food, water, and easy access to areas where man could not find footing. It was afternoon already and we decided to head down. We both had heavy packs since we were not coming back the following weekend. The trip down was one which required scaling twelve to fifteen foot cliffs using ropes. Finally, we could see the valley floor and struggled to the trail. The walk out was fairly easy and flat. We met Annie and headed back to my car.

The next Friday morning I met Al and Annie at the base of Aspen Highland Ski area. We got a ride from the paint crew to the top of the mountain. Logos Peak is the top of the ski area and the paint crew was finishing the towers. We headed out to the south and soon were on the top of Highland Peak which sits directly south of the ski area. From here we could see all Maroon Creek and the Conumdrum Valley. Pyramid Peak and the Maroon Bells were readily visible across the valley. We could even see into part of Willow Basin where we had been the week before. Directly to our south along the ridge was Hunter and Keefe Peak. There was a knife-like ridge that ran directly south with basins on the east and west. We made our way along the ridge to an area with a small stream bubbling out of the hillside. We decided to camp here. After the tents were up and coffee on the fire, we noticed a musky smell. I crept toward it. I soon found myself witnessing one of the wonders of nature.

A herd of about sixty elk occupied a small basin to the south of our camp. The largest six point bull stood in the shade and took on all challengers. A few made half-hearted charges, but the master quickly put them in their place. They bugled all morning. It was hard to leave this magnificent sight, but we wanted to check some of the basins to the east.

We walked along a narrow trail always looking down since we were only about a hundred yards under the ridge. By late in the afternoon we decided to head back to camp and get to bed early, then to put in a long day tomorrow. We had about three miles of tough walking in the morning to reach the base of Hunter Peak.

We were up early; the weather was warm and dry. We headed back along the narrow trail, passing the area we had reached the day before. We continued until we got to the base of Hunter Peak. Although we were able to find fresh sign, we glassed all day without seeing a single sheep. We had seen ewes and lambs before in the area but now they were nowhere to be found. We stayed till the sun was setting in the west over Pyramid Peak. Next morning we were up early again and on the ridge line. We glassed to the south and east again without any luck.

Soon we noticed a band of sheep just a short distance to the north in a small basin. We crept along the ridge line out of site to an area just above and downwind. Here we set up the spotting scope and looked them all over. The largest ram in the band was a two or three year old with horns that were only one-quarter curl. We watched with fascination how they fed around this extremely steep slope and finally bedded on small outcroppings of level ground. They were no more than one-half mile behind the ski area top. About noon we decided, since we had such a long walk out, to make our way down the steep avalanche shoot to Conumdrum Creek. It took us most of the afternoon with the final few hundred yards in a torrential downpour.

Having only two more weekends left of the season, Al and I decided to head back to East Snowmass Creek. We'd already seen most of the rams in this area and felt our chances were better at seeing a legal ram elsewhere. We shouldered our packs at the East Snowmass Creek trailhead Thursday afternoon and by early evening Al, Annie, and I were sitting around the campfire enjoying a spectacular star-filled evening.

During the night the wind picked up dramatically. This worried us. After breakfast we headed up to the ridge line fighting the wind the whole way. By the time we reached the top, it was blowing forty to fifty miles an hour. It was hard to look over the top without shielding your face. We had found some small caves on the east side before and now took shelter in them. The wind was blowing from west to east so when we looked over the ridge into the basins we were looking directly into the wind. We spied some rams and set up the spotting scope. The wind was blowing so hard that the spotting scope was blurry on the lowest power. We saw three rams and could not figure out why we couldn't find the fourth.

This preconceived thinking cost us later. We were sure this was the same band of rams we had seen before with only one legal ram. This time we worked our way to the right directly above the sheep and behind a steep rock outcropping. The wind covered any noise and smell we might have made because it was gale force directly from the sheep to us. We

I was not going to let the cape and horns out of my sight
so I took them with me and headed home.

crossed the only open area we had to cover and soon were behind some steep rocks. We made our way down about one hundred yards and still had not spotted the sheep. Finally, we came to an area where we could sit in the cover of the rocks and watch.

Slowly working his way back to the shelter of the steep crevices was a legal ram. Since we had not seen the fourth ram we figured we should not wait to see all the rams in case they spooked. I was approximately seventy five yards directly above the ram. One shot from the .300 Weatherby sent him tumbling down the steep slope. Not to our surprise, a smaller ram ran to cover on our right. Then as we started to descend, a larger one ran to the right. We kicked ourselves for not waiting. This ram was significantly bigger than the one I had shot and we could only wish him good luck as he disappeared into the steep crevices. What we had not considered was that this was a completely different band.

After pictures and caping, we deboned the meat, put it in a backpack, and headed down the slope to main Snowmass Creek. We had told Annie if she saw us kill the sheep to head back to camp and walk out the other way. There was no way with the weight of the sheep we could have made it up the slope in the wind. The horns and cape weighed about forty pounds and the meat added more. When we came to the cliffs we lowered each other over on ropes, then hit the trail to the car. The walk was fairly long and heavy. But my thoughts were on the third leg of the grand slam I had just completed and what a wonderful experience it had been! It was very exciting to have completed this within forty miles from my residence.

I took the horns straight to the taxidermist where we called the Colorado Division of Wildlife to come over and punch them. This drilling and punch system has cut down on the ability of the poacher to sell illegally taken animals. My ram was the largest to come out of area 13E that year.

The feeling one gets after such extreme physical and mental stress (I lost fifteen pounds in the process) is truly a...

ROCKY MOUNTAIN HIGH.

We made our way to where the ram had come to rest
about fifty yards down the steep slope.
Now the celebration could begin.

8

Jackson Hole Moose

By this time I had started attending the Safari Club International Conventional and Foundation of North American Wild Sheep Convention. Not only is this the F.A.O. Schwartz for adults but if you want to hunt a specific species, a lot of information is available. I was looking for a bighorn sheep hunt in Wyoming, when I met Ron Platt of Encampment, Wyoming. When I didn't draw a sheep permit in Wyoming, but did in Colorado, we still kept in touch. We had talked about a Shiras moose permit. Ron had no moose in his area, but he suggested using Triangle X Ranch of Jackson, Wyoming. I wrote them and learned that the hardest part of getting a moose was drawing a permit. They said, however, Area 14 where they had their elk camp had been successful for the last twenty five years.

More information arrived and I learned that the three Turner brothers' ranch was one of the last left inside the confines of the park. Harold explained the odds were a one-in-fifteen chance of drawing a moose permit in this area. The applications had to be in Cheyenne by March 15.

The information from the Turners indicated they had a very successful operation for their elk hunters. They succeeded over eighty percent of the time from 1969 to 1981. The previous season yielded a ninety-five percent success on elk and a hundred percent on moose. Their dad had built their camp in the Teton Wilderness area in the thirties. It became one of the most successful camps for elk in North America.

Much to my surprise, I drew a Shiras moose permit the first year I applied. I hoped beginner's luck would carry into the hunt. I sent my deposit and the dates of October 9th through the 18th were allotted for the hunt. Harold assured me hunting in their area was great equestrian sport. He advised me to do a lot of riding over the summer. The weather that time of year is very unpredictable but the camps were quite comfortable. The camps consisted of large sidewall tents where the hunters slept off the ground. A fully equipped cook tent supplied breakfast as well as dinners. Hunters usually had lunch on the trail. Horse wranglers and plenty of pack mules and mountain-wise riding horses insured the hunter well-rested, sound stock. It sounded like my hunts of previous years with Gary Powell of Big Nine Outfitters.

October soon arrived and I drove from Glenwood to Jackson Hole. I'd visited the area before on a skiing vacation. I had seen lots of moose and the famous Jackson Hole elk herd in the National Elk Refuge. From Glenwood I drove north to Interstate 80, then west to Rock Springs. Here I turned north through Pinedale and on into Jackson. There had been a bad snowstorm a few days before and by the time I got to the Wort Hotel, I was ready for the prime rib dinner. Charlie, the Texas oilman, was hunting elk at the same time but was delayed and we missed each other.

Next day I visited the galleries and then drove out to the ranch in mid-afternoon. A few other hunters were settling into their cabins to sleep when I finally got there. They gave us each a pannier and asked us to repack our gear. Harold sat all the hunters down and cautioned us to stay in the saddle and keep close to our guide. Some of the shots had to be very quick. It had snowed heavily which made it muddy and bright. I had broken my sunglasses on the way so I drove back to town and bought another pair. I also decided to buy a pair of Sorels since I had left mine at home. I hoped the food at camp was half as good as the hearty meal that night.

The Turners had three camps in the Teton Wilderness on the southeast corner of Yellowstone Park. The upper camp was twenty four miles from the trailhead and covered Two-Ocean Plateau which was one of Teddy Roosevelt's favorite hunting areas.

Enos Lake Camp was twelve miles from the base corrals and next to the largest lakes in the Teton Wilderness area. We planned to hunt out of the lower camp eighteen miles from the base corrals at the foot of the famous big game ridge. The camp near the headwaters of the Snake River had been leased by the family since 1938.

The hunters were from all over the U.S.: two from Texas, Florida, and Mississippi, three from New Jersey, and me. They took us to the base corrals at Pacific Creek trailhead in vans. There the youngest brother, John, met us to take us to the lower camp. Seventy five head of stock occupied the base corrals. Soon we had the mules loaded, saddles and scabbards adjusted, and were on our way.

About a hundred yards from the corral my horse went to its knees and rolled over. Luckily I got off and got my rifle and out of the scabbard before the horse rolled on it. The horse stiffened and abruptly quit breathing. It probably died from a heart attack. I hoped this was not a sign of things to come. Soon another horse was saddled and we were on our way.

The eighteen mile ride took most of the day. The scenery was typical Yellowstone with small rushing streams, dense pine forests on the hill side, and small open parks. It was bitter cold. But the elk, deer, and two small bull moose we saw along the way warmed our spirits. I had learned that a short time walking would warm you up, as well as get some of the sore spots worked out, so I alternated riding and walking along the trail. This is an especially good way to start a morning ride when it's cold.

We got to camp about three in the afternoon and saw it had grown larger to accommodate the increased number of hunters. The camp had been built for six but the closing of the upper camp because of the early snows created a need for a camp large enough for ten. Tents were assigned and we stored our gear. Some hunters sighted in their rifles and John started dinner. It consisted of fresh salad, potato, and steak – a gourmet delight. We went to bed early in anticipation of the morning hunt.

We got to camp about three in the afternoon and saw it had grown larger to accommodate the increased number of hunters.

The night turned bitter cold and we awoke with ice everywhere and the temperature two below zero on October 10. We started with the standard hearty breakfast, after which we mounted our horses for the day's ride. My guide was a day late so Mike, one of the wranglers, filled in. We went with John. We headed straight north about four miles to Upper Fox Park where moose sign was plentiful. John spotted a young bull on the side of a hill. We re-entered the narrow part of the stream and his hunter, a Texan, Ray, jumped off the horse, took a quick shot, and missed. The elk disappeared and we decided to stop for lunch.

It was so cold no one could take a nap so Mike and I went back to where Fox Creek headed out of the meadow. From there we could watch a meadow three hundred yards long by a hundred yards wide. The meadow faced north-south and the northern edge was only a few hundred yards from the park border. John took Ray and Leon, both from Texas, straight east to make a loop and end up in Upper Fox Park. We were to meet them for the ride back to camp.

We sat very still and cold from four until seven seeing twelve mule deer, six cow elk, and one coyote. As the light faded, we noticed a large black object step into the distant reaches of the meadow. We glassed to see a large bull moose with very wide horns. The moose wandered straight toward us before heading into the forest at the east edge of the meadow. Mike and I decided on a spot that afforded us cover, a good view of the meadow, and a rest against a tree. We quickly rode the horses to a site below this, dismounted, and raced to our spot. Just as we got there we saw John and the two hunters making their way along the west edge of the meadow. The moose also must have seen or smelled them. He decided to head back toward the park. To do this quickly he crossed part of the meadow. This gave me a quartering shot behind the left shoulder. I fired four times as he crossed the upper meadow. The snow was quite deep. The moose finally staggered, faltered and ended up on this back in the deep snow.

John heard the shots and met us at the kill for pictures. The three of us caped and cleaned the twelve hundred pound animal. We covered it with small pine branches to discourage predators and headed back to camp. It turned bitter cold as the sun set. We were sure the meat wouldn't spoil overnight. We didn't arrive at camp until eleven thirty. The lights were a welcome sight to the trio of weary hunters. The cook had kept dinner hot, which was even more welcome! Leon, the older hunter from Texas, had made a magnificent shot on a five point bull. We celebrated over a hot meal and a *little* bourbon. Totally exhausted we quickly fell into a deep sleep despite the bitter cold.

We slept in a bit the next morning. The hearty breakfast warmed us before we headed out to get the animals. We took the same trail to Upper Fox Park with five pack mules, John, and the two Texans. Jim, my guide, had made it to camp while we were gone the previous day. He joined Mike and me for the work. We reached the moose and the three of us quartered it and cut off the horns. While we were doing this John took two of the mules and retrieved the elk. He returned just as we finished loading our three mules. We headed back to camp with five loaded mules. The slow trip back gave us time to enjoy the scenery. After the meat was unloaded, we measured the horns. I had set my lower limit of forty inches

He was an exceptional Shiras and in fact turned out to be the
largest taken that year.

in width since this was a smallest of the three moose species. I already had a sixty nine inch Alaskan-Yukon moose and a fifty five inch Canadian moose. Much to my surprise and delight, the moose had a spread of just over a fifty inches with fairly well developed palms! He was an exceptional Shiras and in fact turned out to be the largest taken that year.

This completed my North American moose trophy collection. Congratulations were plentiful. It was Mike's first guided kill. The fact I had the chance to show him a little about stalking and staying downwind made the hunt even more satisfying to me. I've found on many of my hunts some of the most rewarding times come after the kill. This was especially true of this trip. I had time to get to know the other hunters and the crew.

The next day we were off to the upper camp to remove all the horizontal poles with Daryl and Steve. The new forest service rules allows no permanent structures within the national forest. Upper camp was six miles away by horse through some very scenic country. Due to the heavy snows there was little sign except for moose. We passed a carrion with a bald eagle on it and coyote close by digesting his meal.

We made it to upper camp by ten that morning, then removed all the poles and staked the gates that formed the corral. We winterized the camp by the rules set forth by the forest service and then had lunch. The trip back took us by Phelps Pass which did not look this high from upper camp. It was a quiet ride without seeing much game—a good time to reminisce about the events of the week. When we returned, the camp had three five point elk hanging. We made arrangements to take out a load of meat and horns.

Next morning we packed twelve mules with meat, cape, and horns, and headed out. Daryl, Mike, and I took the twenty head pack string and headed for the trailhead. Leaving camp brought both sadness and joy. The camaraderie of the hunters and the success of the hunt had been great and I hated for it to end. Coming off the plateau was like leaving winter and coming into autumn. The lower meadows had little snow, but each time we crossed Pacific Creek it got a little larger. When we finally broke out of the trees we were looking down the valley at the Tetons. There is no greater feeling than our majestic mountains—snow covered behind green, pine tree-covered forests. The warmth felt good after five days of bitter cold. Each wrangler led six packed mules with me in the middle. Fortunately, we only had two small wrecks along the way.

Each time we crossed Pacific Creek it got a little larger.

We arrived at the trailhead about mid afternoon and met Roy Ostermuller of Frontier Taxidermy. He took all the meat and the horns and capes. The meat processing would be done in Dubois. The horns and capes were taken to Cheyenne for the hunters. The van took us all to the ranch where a warm shower and a delicious meal made sleep come easy.

The next morning I explored some of the smaller lakes and trails within the park. To my amazement I was virtually alone. This contrasts to other times I've visited in the summer when it is impossible to be alone anywhere in the park. I even made a side trip to see Old Faithful and it only took a few hours with little traffic. This is a great time to see the park if you want to do it alone.

The trip back through Wyoming was a time to reflect on the Triangle X experience. There can be no doubt this is one of the best run horse outfits in the country. With one hundred head of horses and one hundred fifty head of mules, their

There is no greater feeling than our majestic mountains—snow covered
behind green, pine tree-covered forests.

capabilities are staggering. The organization is excellent and
a trip with them can only be a wonderful experience. My hat
will always be off to Harold, John, and Donald.

9

Tuktu –
a Tale of Two Caribou

Unlike the other stories in this book, this one begins in September of 1983 and doesn't end until September of 1985. I had already collected a mountain caribou trophy with Gary Powell (Big Nine Outfitters) and a Barren Ground with Gary LaRose on the Alaskan Peninsula. Due to the fairly high cost of airfare to the east coast, I decided to get the remaining two caribou in one trip. I would have to hunt the Quebec-Labrador in Quebec because no nonresident permits were issued in Labrador. I would hunt woodland caribou in Newfoundland. (Since then the Central Canada B.G. and Peary [Arctic Island] species have been added.)

I had started a SCI Chapter the year before and felt this would be a great chance to go on a group hunt. I met Gerry Poitras of Tuktu in Quebec and read the rave reviews of his outfit, so I decided on his Tuktu Camp located on the famous George River. Four members of our newly formed Upper Colorado River chapter and four other friends made up the team. All previous reports indicated the hardest part of the hunt would be in getting the caribou to move so you could pick the one you wanted! I arranged with Roland Reid of

Newfoundland and Labrador Outfitters Limited to hunt the next week for woodland caribou.

We flew from Denver to Chicago, picked up our remaining two members, then on to Montreal. We had to stay overnight because the planes arrive in the evening and the one for Shefferville doesn't leave until morning. We found Schefferville is the end of the road—both for auto and rail. The large coal mines in the area have kept it open. With the price of coal down the town was in a bad economical slump. We stayed overnight in Tuktu's trailer house, flew into the lodge on the George River then the next morning. The comfortable camp had a cook and bunks to keep you dry. The weather was warm for this time of year and the news was that the continued warm front had slowed the caribou movement. Across the river was a large hill and on the other side a lake which the caribou forded in their migration. The caribou spent summers on the Labrador coast using the ocean breezes to keep the flies off. Then they migrated inland to a windslope plain to winter. The relentless northern wind does not allow the snow to cover their food supply.

The comfortable camp had a cook and bunks to keep you dry.

Next morning we ferried across the river to the base of the large hill. We split up and covered most of the back side of the lake. Nearly everyone saw caribou that day. Jerry Bachmann took a nice bull that opening morning. Jerry's kill made spirits run high, we thought we had just seen the start of the migration. It evidently was the end, however, because as the days went by we saw fewer and fewer caribou. The weather was very warm and nothing moved. It did allow us time to wonder about all the rock and water which made up most of this country. We took a lot of pictures of non-trophy caribou.

The next day, two of us changed to a lake camp where the caribou were thought to be moving. This proved a mistake. The guide only spoke French and had no apparent interest in hunting. Each day he took us down to the lake and placed us on a trail where caribou had worn a path deep into the wet moss. However, none passed. Another member of the party killed a respectable bull off the river on the third day. Finally on the fifth day we went back to the river camp where we celebrated with a final night dinner. The camp was closing due to ice they told us. We found no ice—only very hot weather. We were promised refunds or credits for another hunt, but left disappointed at only two out of eight hunters getting caribou.

We went back through Wabash and Sept-Isle on the way to Montreal. Here I said goodbye and got on a plane to Halifax and then on to Deer Lake. Roland Reid met me and took me to their home situated seven miles past Cornerbrook. The food was excellent. He showed me on the map where we would fly in the morning. Buchans Plateau was a large expanse of inland country with good numbers of caribou, moose, and black bear. The woodland caribou spend their summers and fall on the plateau before migrating to the coast where the winds keep the snow off their food supply.

As soon as the dew was off the plane the next morning, Roland fired it up and we took off from the river's surface and headed inland. We crossed the timber cuts and roads that traversed back and forth through the pine forests before climbing onto the plateau where there were not any roads. From the air it looked a lot like northern British Columbia with gravel bars on the river beds and a lot of marsh areas for moose. This terrain had less trees and looked very marshy. We landed at Saviour Lake Lodge. The year before the roof caved in under twenty feet of snow. They had rebuilt it about a month before to accommodate this year's hunters. The area was missing the ground rock so prevalent in Quebec. We unloaded the plane and I met my guide, Steven. He was a native Newfoundlander and had been with Roland for five years.

Camp Newfoundland

I was anxious to see some game since Quebec had been so disappointing. After lunch we headed out in the drizzle to climb the large hill behind the camp. We got on top and were able to watch two drainages from this point. We saw thirty to forty caribou and a black bear that afternoon. My spirits lifted knowing the caribou were active and moving. At dark we headed back to camp for a wonderful meal with homemade apple pie. The other hunters had been there a week. They were leaving the next day with four moose. This left Steve and I alone at the camp. Roland was moving the other guides to accommodate the next group of hunters.

In the morning we were off again in hip boots since the terrain was soggy and wet. We climbed the hill and got into position to see a very large herd coming down and across to our left. We stalked to within one hundred yards of the animals and set up the spotting scope to look them over. It's nice to be in an area where you can turn down trophy heads knowing that the next hour or day might bring better ones to look over. For the first time I saw some caribou that had no palmation and horns similar to an elk. Scoring caribou can be very difficult but the rule of thumb is to start at the top and work down. If the top points are few and short, no matter how good the bez and shovels are, it does not score well. After spending all afternoon evaluating the members of this herd we decided to pass and work our way back to camp.

As usual the meal was delicious and sleep came easily. The next day we were stuck at camp in the morning due to rain but spent the afternoon high on the hill glassing open meadows on both sides. The rain stopped by evening but it turned cold and nothing was moving. The cabin felt especially good that night. We could dry our rain-drenched clothes. In front of the fireplace I learned Steve had fished and logged his entire life. He talked about the long winters, large amounts of snow, and the long gray days. Next morning after the heaving dew lifted we started up the hill behind the cabin. When we got to the first bench out of the trees we always stopped to glass the plain in front of us across the lake. This day we saw two big bulls with flowing white manes speeding across the plain. Steve thought they would be out of sight soon but I asked him to set up the scope to take a better look. The bulls topped anything we had seen. One had longer beams but the second had it all—tops, bez, and a double shovel.

Since we were above them we decided we could keep them in sight during the stalk. They were out in the open so the shot would be a long one. Running in hip boots is *real* work and with the rain gear on we were soon sweating profusely. It paid off though. We were now within two hundred yards of the caribou. The bad part was we now had no height advantage. The bulls decided that we were a curiosity and slowed to watch us approach. At about one hundred and fifty yards they got nervous so we sat down and set up the spotting scope. The smaller bull was as spectacular as we originally thought.

The problem was he stood behind the one with longer, spindly horns. We figured if they bolted the bull I didn't want would cover my trophy bull. Finally they calmed down and started to feed. When they separated I pulled down on the bull I wanted and dropped him with two shots. The second bull did not want to leave his friend, but finally as we approached he plodded off through the wet moss as if he were on a paved highway.

We worked our way through mid-calf water to find the trophy. We took many pictures because he was truly a good one. Although the woodland caribou has the smallest horns of the four types, it also has the largest body. We caped and quartered the animal before going for the boat to get it back across the lake. We carried the quarters to the boat and made our way across the lake to camp. Steve worked on the cape. After a hearty lunch we rested in the warmth of the cabin. It's always a good idea to bring a few good books along and this was my time to use them. Roland showed up the next morning in a Jet-Bell Helicopter to take us back to his house. It was an exciting ride with the caribou strapped to the side. We saw a lot of game on the trip back to Cornerbrook.

The next day I contacted Gerry Poitras back at Tuktu, who said the weather was getting colder. He figured there would be a good chance of taking a caribou. After some talking to the airlines I got a reroute through Goose Bay to Wabash where I would overnight before making it back to Schefferville.

Roland and I toured Cornerbrook and the surrounding territory before heading back to Deer Lake to catch my plane. I found out during these conversations that his son lived less than sixty miles from me in Vail, Colorado. He outfitted for deer and elk in the fall, like his dad, and worked for a ski area in the winter.

I returned to Shefferville to find the weather unchanged. I flew into one of the exclusive camps Gerry had set up on a large lake in the area. We flew to Frontier Camp which was north and east of the previous George River Camp. The camp was a delight with hot showers every night, wine with dinner, and a guide for each hunter.

My highlight of the next four days was meeting and talking to the Shah of Iran's brother HRH Prince Abdorreza Pahlavi.

Here on the ground was the trophy I had waited three years
for and made four trips to bag. It had everything—
long top points, good bez, and an excellent shovel.

He had won the 7th Weatherby award in 1962 for the out-standing hunter of the year. We talked a lot about his home-land and the five species of sheep it contained. There were seven other hunters in camp and each morning we would get into large canoes and head down the lake to a spot where the caribou crossed. Here we would climb high to the ridge line and glass and glass—to no avail.

The weather didn't change and the caribou weren't moving. After four days we all left, unhappy about the fact we got no trophies. I returned home to think of the moonscape which we hunted with all the rock and water—only to yearn to return. Since the weather was a problem, two of us decided to go back the following year for the last of the regular hunts. They assured us the caribou were moving and that this was *the* season for trophy bulls. What we didn't know was that this largest herd in North America was migrating on a more north-erly route. This took the largest percentage of the herd outside of Gerry's area.

Next September Tom Phillippe and I naively headed back to Schefferville and Tuktu. A night in Montreal prior to the trip north was a lot of fun. In Schefferville Tuktu met us, took us to the airplane, and flew us to Frontier Camp. The flight brought back memories of rocks and water as we headed for this desolate wilderness. The landing strip was clear and we saw a few racks laying on the runway as we landed. Seven of the eight departing hunters had scored. Still they were not happy because very few caribou were seen and they had to shoot the first decent one they saw. When we entered the camp the guides were still depressed about the last season. We begun to suspect the main migration had not come through as usual. That meant they were scrambling to find their clients a shootable caribou.

It was very warm, but that night the wind picked up and it turned cool. The next morning excitement was in the air, for this was the first change in the weather this season. Maybe lady luck would shine on us. The lake was about ten miles long and one mile wide. Due to the gusting wind we decided to go north to the end of the lake about a mile away. The big canoes were the same as last year and soon we were at the edge of the water. Here we got out and hiked up a long valley with a wide expanse and no end. We reached the top only to gaze over into a longer valley. We had walked two miles to the top and had not crossed a fresh track in the snow. It was a good place to glass except for the forty mile an hour wind. Soon we had to head for cover. We made it back to shore just in time to notice the waves were cresting with white caps in the middle of the lake. The guide told us we should head for camp because this indicated a big storm was on the way.

We did not realize, as we had gone north, that we were traveling with the wind. Heading home we were going directly into the wind. We stuck to the shoreline but still had to beach about one-half mile from camp and walk back. We laughed about the fact as we had a hot shower and sat down to dinner.

What we didn't realize at first was that one party hadn't made it back to camp. The storm roared and temperatures fell below zero. We knew the party had two guides with them and would be safe but it still concerned us. Next morning fulfilled our fears. Due to the high waves they could not get across the lake without fear of capsizing. Tuktu had a helicopter but it was unable to fly due to strong winds. All that day and the next we were unable to go out except for brief periods due to the cold. Finally, on the third day the storm cleared. It was still cold but no wind.

Early that morning the two hunters made it back to camp after a harrowing experience. They had spent two nights out although they kept warm and dry by using a lean-to and a large fire. The two French-Canadian guides had both trapped in the winter and knew how to live in the icy north. We left them to shower, eat, and sleep. We took the boats and headed down the lake. We couldn't believe our eyes. Everywhere the water had splashed on the shore or rocks it had frozen! It looked like running water coming out of the rocks. We spent that day and the next looking for a caribou. No one in the camp saw a living caribou after the storm. We had gone from two weeks of the warmest weather they had seen to the coldest.

We packed our gear and headed home. On the way we stopped at Mistibini Camp only to find that they had experienced similar failure. Of the sixteen hunters not one had killed a caribou. On the way home Tom and I discussed that even though we had a good offer to return, we would pass. Next time we would go somewhere else.

That somewhere turned out to be a pleasant surprise. After much research we realized that the northern camps had been very successful compared to the southern camps in Quebec. The herd had migrated to the north either due to pressure or just variation of their time honored routes. We met with Fred Webb who told us he was opening a third camp at Weymouth Bay Inlet on the east side of Ungava Bay. This was their northern-most camp and we could shoot two caribou if we got the chance. Since on three separate occasions we hadn't seen a shootable bull, this excited us. We called a few references and soon had our deposit in Fred's hands.

Since we were to be about five hundred miles north of Shefferville we decided to go on earlier dates. Some of the caribou would still be in velvet but we wanted the most active dates for caribou movement.

Tom and I met in Chicago and went on to Montreal. We laughed about the fact even the girl's faces looked familiar. Here our trip took a different course. Instead of going north and east we flew straight north to Fort Chimo—or as the Inuit called it "Kuujjuaq." We had to wait at the airfield for the twin Otter to return. Soon we loaded and were on our way, flying over the Payne and across flat country. Going north we flew over the two other camps Tunulik and Akuliaq. We crossed the George River as it empties into the bay and noticed with the tide out we could see about one hundred yards of bank normally covered with water. The tide in this area ranges from thirty five to fifty feet. When we approached Weymouth Bay Inlet we could see the long finger heading inland. We circled the strip and were soon on the ground. Five hunters were leaving and all had exceptional caribou. We watched the plane take off, hoping our third time would be the charm.

One of the crew showed us to our comfortable tents. The walls were plywood while the roof was tent material. Each had a Coleman oil stove in the middle and foam rubber mattresses. We unpacked and headed for the cook tent. Here we met our guides, Tom's and my guide was Joe. Joe moved his family here for the hunting season. He was older and assured us we would see caribou. I had read about the white bulls of Ungava and couldn't wait to see one. Next morning after a wonderful breakfast we boarded the boats. We noticed the tide was out and the boats further away than the night before. The Indians told us the highest reported tide was a staggering seventy-two feet.

We crossed the inlet and made our way a few miles inland before turning into a small cove. Here we saw multiple small bands of large bull caribou. We beached the boat and stalked to within two hundred yards of the largest group. It was amazing to see the heads bobbing with the heavy racks. Taking no chances on a weather change, I picked out what I thought was the largest. Shooting sixty degrees uphill, I downed him with one shot. The climb to get to him was straight up — but the result was worth it. Here on the ground for and made four trips to bag. It had everything —
long top points, good bez, and an excellent shovel. Here on the ground was the trophy I had waited three years for and made four trips to bag. It had everything — long top points, good bez, and an excellent shovel. I was extremely happy because this was my fourth caribou. We caped and quartered the animal and carried it back to the beach. We found the boat fifty yards up on shore — while we had left it at the water's edge. We cruised the bay and Tom looked over many large bulls but saw none to his liking. Finally in late afternoon we headed back to camp where Joe took the head to finish caping. Tom and I headed for the cook tent.

The next morning after breakfast we headed the other way toward Ungava Bay. We turned off into a second inlet which took us along the coast. Here we saw white bulls standing along the shoreline high in the rocks. Soon we realized that about eighty percent of the caribou we saw were large bulls. That afternoon we made our way to a more sheltered inlet that we could get to only during high tide. For a narrow area the water was like a rushing river it first filled, then emptied, the inlet. We had lunch, set up the scope, and I spotted an exceptionally wide caribou in the distance. He walked over the horizon but didn't spook. I'd vowed not to take my second caribou until Tom took one so it was his turn. We took the boat to get a closer look. After beaching and a short stalk up the hill, Tom anchored the caribou with one shot. The bull measured sixty inches across and was completely white except for black leggings. The main beams were palmated but the size and bulk of the rack was very impressive. When we returned to camp the other hunters had all taken their first caribou. The only hunter without would take just one the entire hunt.

The third day we were up and in the boat early. The weather had progressively worsened almost from the time we arrived. First rain, then snow with the temperature hovering in the 32 to 35 degree range and strong winds out of the northwest. We continued with four hour hunts in the morning, followed by lunch, then four-hour hunts to close the day. We worked the inlets glassing the sides of these relatively steep slopes. It was quite different from the area we hunted before with its flat terrain. We saw large bulls along the breaks and ridges of these inlets. With the pressure off the third afternoon we made our way back into the drainage of a large basin. We sat down and watched a large herd of caribou work toward us. Over the next few hours we saw at least three hundred filing past us in an orderly fashion. One even laid his head down about one hundred yards from us and took a nap. I used two rolls of film and spent one of the most enjoyable days I have ever experienced. We finally ran out of film and headed back to camp.

Early the fourth day we headed back to the coast but saw few caribou. We did stalk one large double shovel which we had seen a few days before in the same area. It was very wide but had poor points on top. We went back to the boat for lunch and moved to the inlet where we took the first caribou. Once again feeding uphill toward a pass, we noticed a large wide caribou. He was two hundred yards ahead of us. We thought we could get closer. As in my previous experience in Alaska, we walked and ran as fast as we could and when we were at the top, he was farther away. But now I could sit down for a good rest and see he was feeding slowly with three other bulls and a few cows. After I settled down a few shots put him on the ground. He was much more palmated than the first caribou. However, his points on top were not as long. His bez and shovel were more palmated which made him a classic example of the Quebec-Labrador species. We caped and

After he dried and scored, he ranked number four
in the SCI Record Book.

carried him back up the hill to the boat. On top of the hill we literally ran into a herd of twenty five bulls. Tom took the largest double shovel in the group.

We arrived at camp late but happy. Everyone had filled out including the gentleman from Minnesota who only wanted to take one. We celebrated at dinner that night and made plans to get out one day early. By midday the fifth day the meat was boxed. The capes and horns were ready for travel.

His bez and shovel were more palmated which made him a classic example of the Quebec-Labrador species.

The plane arrived in the early afternoon. After a short stop in the town of George River to drop off some of the passengers we took off for Fort Chimo. We spent the night in Fort Chimo before heading back to Montreal and home. I'll never forget the looks of the other hunters at the airport as we unloaded our caribou.

The total trip took only seven days with five days hunting. It was one of the most enjoyable trophy hunting experiences I've ever had. It was nothing to see twenty five bulls in each of the four hour hunts during the day. And the food and accommodations were excellent, despite the remoteness of the camp.

I can't imagine a better bow hunting experience since these caribou migrate in relatively predictable patterns. More than once we were within ten to fifteen yards of a large bull caribou.

The third time was indeed a charm.

10

Alaskan Brown Bear and Salmon

I was sitting in a board meeting of SCI in 1983, complaining to Eric Wagner of Florida about how the price of bear hunts had got out of control. He said he had hunted the previous year with an outfitter who was reasonable and produced good bears. The hunts are on the southeast coast of Alaska, and although the bears are large they are not in the class of bears taken on Kodiak Island. He was emphatic about hunting the first ten days of September. This was the opening of bear season and the streams were still full of salmon, both of which contribute to a successful hunt. The season lasted the whole month but due to hunting pressure and the fish disappearing from the stream, it made sense to go early. I dashed off a letter to A. J. Israelson of Yakutat, Alaska and asked about the details of his hunts.

In days of word processors and computers it's comforting to get a handwritten letter. All of the old fraternity of outfitters: Gary Powell, Gary LaRose, Len Pickering, and A.J. communicate via handwritten letters.

Later, I learned A.J. Israelson was one of the master guides of Alaska, a status not equaled by many. He explained there were no openings for the first dates in 1983, but if I could wait until 1984 the dates were free. I wrote back and booked 1984. I talked to Eric more in the months before the hunt and he passed along a few tips. He also advised me to take a fishing pole.

John Johnson, the administrator of the hospital where I do most of my work, expressed an interest in going. Another letter to A.J. and we were both booked to go. He explained in the following letters that there was service daily between Yakutat and Seattle due to the heavy sport fishing in the area.

John wanted to look for a mountain goat if he had time but I wanted a nice bear. I planned to focus on one between seven and eight feet. A.J. had informed us the bear population was excellent but few bears were over nine feet. He told us to arrive in Yakutat on the thirty first of August. We would purchase our licenses and fly to camp so we could start on opening day.

The time passed slowly. Finally the end of August arrived and we were on our way to Seattle. Early next morning we were headed north, stopping at Sitka and Juneau before landing at Yakutat. The weather was gloomy and rainy but the 737 landed without a hitch. Gary Gray met us. He had since taken over A.J.'s area. After buying the licenses, we met with A.J. who took us to the air strip. The plane was already loaded. We noticed that the fuel tanks surrounding the field all had A.J.'s name on them. Later we learned he owned the Exxon distributorship. Every engine—whether boat, plane, or auto—used his oil and gas. His son ran the distributorship. That left time for A.J. to hunt a little, then winter in Hawaii.

Soon we were flying straight south from Yakutat. I had landed in Kodiak once but had only flown over this area on my trips to Anchorage. The southeast coast of Alaska is a truly beautiful area. The mountains are very close to the shoreline and the glaciers empty into streams which wind a short distance to the ocean. We were going to hunt at Dry Bay just south of the Alsek River. This was very close to Glacier Bay National Monument, but since A.J. had his permit from almost the beginning of guide era he could hunt in the area. A flat plains spread from the shoreline to the mountains. This expanse was about ten miles and was covered by a lot of willows and Devil's Club. When A.J. first started guiding in this area he said it was mostly grassy plain interspersed with trees.

We circled the cabin and soon were on the ground.

We noticed a fish processing plant on the edge of the peninsula just before landing. We unpacked in a very comfortable two bedroom cabin and had a wonderful dinner by Mrs. Israelson. Then we planned the next day's hunt. I would hunt with Frank Ingledue and John would go with Gary. We would drive over to the East Alsek River in the morning and then start hunting.

That evening we learned all the vehicles and buildings on the peninsula come here by barge. The barge stopped once a month to unload the freight and pick up anything that needed to go back to Yakutat. A B25 flew in daily to the dirt strip behind the cannery to take the fresh frozen fish through Juneau to Seattle. It was possible to have fish on your table in the states in two days. A.J. said a lot had changed in the twenty seven years he had guided this area. The area was now in the Glacier Bay National Preserve.

Early the next morning we loaded the Toyota gear and headed down the peninsula to the fish plant. Here the East Alsek River emptied into a long marsh-like area and then a channeled into the ocean. The Alsek was three hundred yards wide and very swift and deep, while the East Alsek was twenty yards wide and varied between pools and shallow rapids.

You could feel the salmon brushing against your hip boots as you entered the water. Frank and I went up stream while John and Gary went down. We walked for about a mile and a half before finding a small area between rapids where we could watch a large pool. We sat here all day without seeing a bear. Meanwhile an exciting story was unfolding a few miles downstream.

John and Gary had ran into a bear a few hundred yards downstream. Thinking it was not as large as they wanted they walked toward it. And the bear swam toward them. It entered the thick bank just as they determined it was indeed very large. They froze in their steps as they heard the bear approaching. After a few tenuous moments it reappeared not more than twenty yards from them and headed their way. John fired first, followed by a volley of bullets which put the bear on the ground for good. The bear squared nine foot four inches. John was justifiably ecstatic. They cleaned and took the hide and skull back to camp. They returned later and when we walked back down the stream to the Toyota we found them waiting smugly. During the drive back to camp, John was so excited he could hardly tell us about the bear's charge. That night we celebrated with a fine meal and hit the bed early.

The September air turned cool as we headed out the next day. John was to stay at camp while they worked on the hide and skull. Later we would learn that John's skull would have made the SCI book except one of the shots racked the back two inches of the skull. On the ride down and across the peninsula we decided to go where John and Gary had gone the previous day. We stopped at the spot and entered the pool. This time we went downstream and found some amazing trails pounded out along the bank where the bears had been fishing. Judging by the amount of bear dung around the bank they gorged themselves. We worked our way down to a large pool where the salmon were thick. Frank and I spent a lot of time talking about the fungus around the salmon's heads that eventually kills them.

The salmon were so thick you thought
you were going to walk on them.

About three in the afternoon we saw our first bear, a seven to eight foot chocolate brown variety. He crossed the river about fifty yards below us. As he entered the bank on our side he must have caught our scent because he growled a few times and headed off into the willows. After he got out of the water he literally disappeared. It was amazing something so big could disappear so quickly. We headed back along the bank to the Toyota. As we turned the last corner a seven and one-half foot bear was standing in the middle of the stream trying to catch our scent. He noticed some movement and disappeared in a flash. It was becoming obvious there were plenty of bears in that area and if we were patient, we should be able to find a large one. The salmon were still heading inland to spawn. When we came to the rapids where the water was only a few inches deep, you could literally catch the fish with your hands. They made a swishing sound as they went from one pool to the next.

We returned to camp to learn the bad news about John's skull. The hide was cleaned and salted. Proper care of bear hides is very important since hair slippage is common and ruins the mount. The spotting scope was set up and John was glassing the far mountain for goats. They planned to cross the Alsek in the morning and climb the mountain for a look at the higher reaches. At dinner we talked about the two bears we had seen. We decided the next day we would take a canoe with us. Frank told us some stories about hunting bears off large boats in and around the ABC's. We had not heard of this acronym but learned he was talking about Admiralty, Baranof, and Chichagof Islands. They used large luxury cruisers to tour the many bays and inlets then made the final stalk on the shoreline.

Next morning we were up early, had a hearty breakfast, tied the canoe on top of the Toyota, and headed for the East Alsek. We unloaded the canoe, put our gear in it, and started upstream. The canoe was surprisingly stable in the pools. And it was easy to carry it up the shallow rapids. We watched the largest pool most of the day but went to the uppermost pool for the later afternoon. We saw a dark eight foot sow with two light cubs frolicking in a small pool a few hundred yards away. We took some pictures and watched in awe as she would catch a fish, drag it to shore, and while it was flapping around, the cubs would pounce on it. Such is the way of teaching in nature. As the afternoon wore on we decided to start back. We were going to canoe about three miles past the Toyota to the mouth of the river which formed a large marshy area before leaving.

Going by the second pool we noticed for the third consecutive day the larger openings in the wall of willows where the bears were coming out to feed. We commented that one of these days we should watch this area a little more closely. Nothing in the next two pools. Just as we turned the final corner into the marshy area, we noticed some waterfowl that looked like they had just taken off. We spotted a seven to eight foot bear making his way along the shoreline in search of food. We took some pictures. The bear never spooked but methodically made his way past us. We finally beached the canoe by a fishing lodge. Frank walked back to get the Toyota. It was dark as Frank appeared. Putting the canoe on the vehicle, we headed home.

The lights lit only a narrow path as we headed back to camp. Soon we could see the distant camp lights and knew a warm meal and bed would be waiting. We hit the door with the stories of the two bears we had seen and noticed John and Gary weren't very interested. They had already eaten and were about to go to sleep. We could not figure out why they were so tired. Then John told us of the long climb they had made to the top of the mountain and how their feet had not fared well. John developed some blisters on the way down that would keep him in camp for the next few days. A day in leather boots after the days we had been having in waders made a lot of difference. The bed felt good and I could not help but wonder if we were getting closer to seeing the big one.

Next day we were back at the East Alsek early, putting in the canoe and heading upstream. By now we could easily portage the rapids. We complemented each other rowing so the trip took us to the uppermost pool in short order. We pulled the canoe on shore and found a grassy spot to sit and watch the long pool. The day was warm and the waterfowl would stop for awhile on their way south. After lunch it was so warm I took a nap. I awoke to find Frank glassing the shoreline.

About two in the afternoon an eight to eight and one-half foot bear started fishing just above where we had seen the sow and two cubs the day before. At first we thought he was not large enough but after continued glassing we settled on nine feet so we thought we'd better get a closer look. He caught a fish and took it out of sight, so it was time to move closer. We made our way quietly up the back to a spot opposite the pool. We sat down in the willows and waited. We were about twenty yards away from the pool. Both of us were a little tense about being so close. We were sitting in thick willows and a hasty retreat would be tough.

After a few minutes the sow appeared with her two cubs remaining on the bank. She splashed into the pool after a fish but must have gotten a whiff of our scent because she immediately stood up, looked our way, and growled. She snarled and growled as she left as if we had chased her out of her favorite fishing spot. Soon afterward we heard another set of growls. They sounded a lot deeper and we figured with the afternoon wind swirling our scent had carried to the boar. We sat quietly for a few more minutes before becoming disappointed and going back to the canoe. We pulled it back into the water and headed downstream.

As we shot out of the first rapids we noticed a large black object fishing at the far end of the pool. The bear was four hundred yards away but Frank noted he could not see light under the bear's belly and that his head looked small in comparison to his body. The bear was fishing where we had seen the large openings in the wall of willows and we knew the water there was only a few inches deep. It was quite dark on the tree side of the pool and Frank headed the canoe quietly toward the bear. The closer we got the bigger the bear looked in the dim light. On all fours he covered about one third of the stream. There was a small island about seventy five yards from the bear that would offer us a little cover. We slowly made our way toward it keeping our eyes glued on the bear. Just as we were getting close the bear caught a fish and disappeared in the underbrush.

As we got closer to the island the bottom of the aluminum started scraping the bottom. I put one foot out to stop the boat. Hearing the noise the bear came back to the stream. As Frank steadied the canoe I placed the crosshairs on the left front shoulder for a quartering shot. The .300 Weatherby roared in the stillness and all I detected was a slight flinch on the part of the bear. It turned and disappeared in the alders through the large hole we had noticed previously. We quickly got over to the area where the bear was standing and saw on the bank where he had fed on fish. It was almost dark now and Frank did not want to enter the alders for fear of a wounded bear. It had not appeared to be badly wounded. I didn't want to leave but saw as it got darker we couldn't look without putting ourselves in danger. We pulled the canoe over the rapids and floated to the next pool. We saw two more bears in the fading light. They splashed their way to shore as we made our way back to the Toyota.

By the time we got to the Toyota it was dark and we headed back to camp. Frank asked over and over if I had hit the bear. All I could say was I had a good sight pattern and from that close I didn't think I could miss. The Weatherby's noted for its punch and has always been my most trusted rifle. I hoped it had done its job. We arrived at camp excitedly blurting out the story. We had a muted celebration and made plans for four of us to search the area in the morning. Frank had told Gary and A. J. the size of the bear and both lectured us about being very careful. I found it tough to sleep that night. My worst nightmare would be if I wounded the bear and it got away, only to suffer and die later. All true hunters would rather miss outright than wound a game animal.

Finally morning came and we continued to plan over breakfast. A.J. said he would go aloft in the plane in case the wounded bear spooked. This way he might be able to see movement we could not see on the ground. We put the canoe in at the same spot and soon were pulling it up the rapids where I had shot the bear. We waited until A.J. was overhead and headed into the alders. The day was bright. We had already found a few drops of blood on the bank we couldn't see in the dusk the night before. As we entered the alders the light went from bright sunshine to almost dark. We stayed in

In the closed space of the alders the bear looked immense.
John commented that it resembled a Volkswagen with hair.

pairs and followed the paths worn down by the feeding bears. Frank and Gary went to the left and John and I headed right.

After fifty yards we came to a large blood spot in the trail. As we looked up we saw a huge mound of dark brown hair ahead. We yelled to Gary and Frank and soon they were at our side. The bear was on all fours as if he were sleeping. There was no movement and we could see another spreading pool of blood close by.

Now was the time to celebrate. We yelled and pounded each other on the back. Gary ran out to wave to A.J. and we heard the plane move off toward the cabin. We took many pictures and then went to work skinning. It took all four of us just to roll him over. After three hours we carried the hide to the canoe and returned to the Toyota. This time as we headed back to camp we celebrated the whole way. We took more pictures at camp and even A.J. got excited. He said considering the size of the head, this may be the largest bear he had taken in the area. Gary worked on the hide as I told the story over and over! I now knew the bullet went clean through the bear's chest before coming to rest under the hide on the opposite side. He probably died within seconds of entering the alders. We rested the remainder of the day. That evening after salting the hide we went down to watch an area where the fish camp dumped the entrails and heads of the fish.

The dump was fenced with an electric fence but the bears just walked right through it to get their meals. We saw two good bears, one about eight and one-half feet with only one ear. The bear had probably lost it in a fight with another bear. He had been spotted every year for the last six years at the dump. It was too dark to take any good pictures so we headed back to camp. The fish camp only processed fish four days because that's all the time they were allotted. The streams had to rest three out of seven days to allow the salmon to spawn. The other reason we went to the dump was that the wolves in the area came there for an easy meal and we wanted to watch them. We went home to a tasty meal and then to bed where sleep came quickly.

Next day we discovered the skull would not even fit into the ten gallon can they usually used to boil them! They had to fashion a new container out of a fifty five gallon drum. We

The next day after the skull had been cleaned it measured twenty seven
and six-eighths! That made it the largest bear taken by A.J.
It squared nine feet eleven inches on the ground.

went back to the dump in the morning for wolves and then on to the mouth of the East Alsek for some salmon fishing. It was fun to catch the twelve to twenty pound salmon on almost every cast. We were only allowed to keep two but they would feed the camp. We encountered one bear out on the mouth that afternoon but stayed clear of him. We were home early for a wonderful meal of fresh salmon. Since we both had taken bears much larger than we expected John and I we were ecstatic. This led to one of those unexpected days I previously alluded to after you had your game and the pressure of the hunt was behind you.

It was fun to catch the twelve to twenty pound salmon on almost every cast. We were only allowed to keep two but they would feed the camp!

The next day turned out even better as A.J. took us on a tour of the area while Frank and Gary tended to the hides and skulls. A.J. had a large speed boat anchored on the Alsek and John and I got a ten mile ride against the raging current to the head of the river. The river came pouring out of a large glacier pool full of floating icebergs. Once in the pool there was very little current. We had lunch where the river came out of Canada and was quite small. The large glacier at the head of the pool emptied its contents of ice into the pool. The large chunks of ice made their way to the mouth of the outlet where they became grounded on the shallow shelf. Here they melted down and then were able to float out into the main current where they entered the river. The pool was quiet and unique. Bald eagles sat on top of the icebergs looking for their next meal. The weather got colder and soon we were heading back to camp with an incredible experience behind us.

The next day after the skull had been cleaned it measured twenty seven and six-eighths! That made it the largest bear taken by A.J. It squared nine feet eleven inches on the ground. We took more pictures and recounted the story several times before thinking about leaving.

Each day we went to the dump but never again got a glimpse of the wolves. One night they howled as if they were coming but never showed. Finally the day to depart arrived. We loaded our gear into the plane. A.J. flew us back to Yakutat along the mountains. Here we got a birds eye view of the glaciers that empty into the ocean. Although a short flight, it was one of the most memorable I've ever taken. We landed and unloaded our gear. Next we took the skulls for the Fish and Game Department to check. They pulled a tooth of my bear and aged it at nine years. Larger bears on Kodiak live to be twenty so this bear had grown remarkably during his nine short years. This was probably due to the abundant supply of salmon available.

We headed to the Yakutat Lodge for a final goodbye and soon had our hides stored in a fish box, ready to board the 737 back to the lower forty eight. On the plane John and I continued to talk about the beauty of the region and the abundance of big bears. This is also one of the only areas of the glacier bear. The glacier bear is a blue-silver color variation of the black bear. Gary had taken one of the larger ones in the area a few years before.

We laid over at Juneau and then went on to Seattle where we over-nighted before returning home. As we got off the plane in Denver *we were two very happy hunters.*

11

Arctic Musk Ox

After my successful bear hunt to Yakutat I was home reading one of my many flyers from Klineburger Worldwide Travel. It said there was room for a party of five to hunt musk ox at Holman, Northwest Territories in the spring. I called, confirmed the dates, and started to round up hunters. My first group hunt for caribou hadn't turned out so well but I found a lot of enthusiasm for this hunt. Soon I had my other four hunters: Tom Phillippe, Jr., Dion Luke, Don Meske, and Alan Baier. All were members of the chapter of Safari Club I had started and served as the current president. Don and Dion were good friends as well as Tom, Alan, and I. Dion, Alan, and I would come from western Colorado, Tom from Indiana, and Don from Pennsylvania.

Sport hunting for musk ox began in 1979 in the Northwest Territories (NWT). Game management officials determined the herds were increasing too fast. Hunting was one way to keep it in check. The largest herds were on the islands of Victoria and Banks. Others were scattered throughout the northern part of the NWT. Hunts mainly originated from Sachs Harbor on Banks Island and Holman on Victoria Island. Paulatuk and Tuktoyaktuk on the mainland were also excellent areas. The herd on Victoria Island numbered thirteen thousand. The terrain is rough with rolling hills to the north and lunar landscapes to the south and east. There are no trees on Victoria Island as it lies three hundred miles north of the Arctic Circle.

The musk ox has resided in North America for ninety thousand years. The changing climate has altered the range of this northern animal. The musk ox roams as far north as Ellesmere Island, Canada's most northerly point, and rarely comes below the timberline. Eskimos call musk ox Oomingmak, or the bearded one. Musk oxen are usually dark brown with long shoulder hair. Beneath the long hair that rings the animal like a skirt is a thick wool called quiviat or oown. The wool is one of the warmest natural fibers known to man. The animal needs this protection from the four months of total darkness where temperatures may reach -60 degrees. Musk ox travel in herds from two to a hundred. When threatened, they form a semicircle with the dominant male in front. It is virtually impenetrable. It's a lucky wolf that ever breaks this line of defense without getting trampled and killed. A large bull will stand over four feet and weigh seven hundred and fifty pounds.

Dion and I met Alan in Grand Junction and boarded a flight to Salt Lake City. We switched planes and were on our way to Edmonton, Alberta. There we met Tom and Don and went to our motel. It had been almost ten years since the first hunt Tom and I had hunted together. We had a lot catching up to do. We spent much of the night talking about the previous hunting seasons. We were at the airport early the next morning, boarded a trusty 737, and headed north. The plane had only half the regular seats because it carried a lot of freight. We flew straight to Yellowknife for a short stop then on to Norman Wells and Inuvik. Here we met Jessie the triage officer for Guided Arctic Expeditions. Five other hunters were on the plane headed to Sachs Harbor.

Inuvik is in the Mackenzie Delta at the end of the line of Canada's Dempster Highway. It was born on July 18, 1958 when the commissioner of the Northwest Territories named the Arctic's newest town. They were looking for a location to serve as a trans-shipping point for the Delta area and for the Beaufort Coast. The town became the jumping off point for the western arctic islands, as well as a cultural and commerce center. Schools and a hospital sprouted and soon plans began for the Dempster Highway.

Jessie took us to town and we checked into a motel. We were soon out sightseeing around the town. Next Jessie took us to get fitted for caribou mukluks, warm down overalls, and a large down coat. We also got caribou or wolf gloves to go over our smaller gloves and an arctic sleeping bag. The down gear is the type used by the oil workers on the north-shore rigs. Many sizes were available and it was easy to fit everyone. We all changed our light garments for the heavy gear.

Next we met the manager of Guided Arctic Expeditions. He filled us in on where we were going and what we would need. The Canadian Government pays the manager's salary to arrange hunts in the various villages. The Eskimos run the hunting of their species like a coop depending on who has the permits. They hunt polar bear, Peary caribou, and Central Canada B.G. caribou, as well as musk ox. That night we dined in one of the best restaurants in town. The choice was surprising. They had everything from lobster to filet mignon.

Next morning Jessie picked us up and took us back to the airport. We boarded a King Air and were on our way. It was hard to imagine how cold it was; everything was white as it had been since we left Yellowknife. Passing over the delta we could see many lakes and channels all frozen solid. Soon we were over the Arctic Ocean. Looking down you could see ice ridges and occasional small breaks in the ice. We spotted the island and could see hills that were up to fifteen hundred feet high. We crossed the Diamond Jenness Peninsula and spotted the strip at Holman. The flight had taken about two hours.

A pickup met us, loaded our gear, and took us to town. The mile and half ride allowed us to talk to some of our guiding crew. They took us to the Arctic Char Inn, a comfortable motel in the middle of town. Here we unpacked and ate again. We learned we were the first hunters since last November. They took us to the NWT Department of Fish and Game. We bought our licenses and tags for the hunt. The organization of the hunt had been excellent so far. All the guides were excited about hunting again. After dinner we sat around a map and made arrangements for morning. Tom and I were to go north and east to converge on a mountain range where the musk ox herded. Dion, Don, and Alan were going to go east and north toward the same destination. Since there were two to a room, Tom and I fell asleep swapping stories from our past hunts.

Next morning we awoke to a hearty breakfast. We were soon in our clothes with all the gear they had given us on the outside. We headed out to meet our guides and help pack the snow machines. We quickly realized we were not going to be much help in the cold. We stood around holding our rifles as they loaded the sleds. The guides worked in pairs with one sled full of supplies and one sled to pull the hunter. Fully loaded, the sled was quite heavy. Within all the gear was a place to sit with our legs out straight. The rider faced backwards, for any exposed part of the skin would immediately freeze. Even then the cold crept in. After a few minutes it became clear why we were using their gear. We said our goodbyes and headed in different directions to meet again that night. The sun was high but you could feel no heat. We crossed the runway and headed straight north. The town faded in the distance and the landscape was like a white desert.

After about an hour of riding the snowmobiles stopped. Before I could get out of the sled the Eskimos had a Coleman burner lit and were making tea. The warm tea felt good. Soon I had to relieve myself, however, and I found out drinking the tea was not such a great idea. It was hard to believe that with a bright blue sky and sunshine it was -35 degrees. It warmed up to -25 about noon. The hoods of the large down parkas covered our head in back and face masks and ski goggles protected the front. Amazingly, the Eskimo drivers wore only sun glasses. Their skin had acclimated over time to withstand the cold.

Soon we ran into a snow storm coming out of the north. Although light, it was hard to see even for a short distance. The sleds stopped again and after a little pow-wow the guides informed us they were going to head back because the storm worried them. Tom and I crawled into the sleds and we took off for Holman. The guides informed us they would make radio contact with the other hunters and find out how the weather had treated them. We found out later Alan's sled had broken down. Don had waited with him for awhile. Dion had gone further inland and was the first to find the herds of musk ox and take one. Don got one that evening. They were south and east enough to have missed the storm and made camp. Tom and I enjoyed another night at the Arctic Char Inn. The bed felt wonderful; I couldn't imagine why I felt so tired. Then I realized the cold really takes a lot out of you.

Next morning was bright and we headed the same direction as the other hunters. We traveled north and west in the morning circling to the south and east by the afternoon. Tom and I marveled at how good the sandwiches and hot tea tasted. After lunch, we spotted our first caribou grazing along a wind swept ridge. We traveled all afternoon finally coming to the mountainous area of the peninsula. Here we slowed down on each ridge and got out the glasses to look at the next ridge. Finally, we spotted three bull musk ox on the horizon. The chase was on. They led us over three ridges before assuming their circle for danger. The agility of these large animals on the steep slopes and ridges was unbelievable. We slowly made our way up to the circle, trying to judge horn mass and length.

The three bulls formed their defensive posture, as Tom and I got into position. My guide had chosen a musk ox opposite Tom's. The guides decided I would shoot first and the remaining two would run toward Tom. Now came the next problem, would my gun fire in this cold temperature? I had instructed the group to degrease their guns and it was time to test the results. I chambered a round and put the cross hairs on the front shoulder. I fired and the musk ox turned toward me in a menacing position. This time I put the cross hairs just under the lower jaw and fired again. As I fired my second shot, Tom fired at his. Two more shots rang out and his was on the ground.

It was starting to get dark and we still hadn't made camp. We quickly took some pictures and headed for a small frozen lake we had crossed chasing the musk ox. Here my guide noticed I had white spots on my face. I'd removed my face mask to take the pictures.

The three guides set up camp and ferried the musk oxen to camp with a snowmobile. The tents were raised between, and tied to, the sleds. We put all the fuel and gear on the side

I fired and the musk ox turned toward me in a menacing position. This time I put the cross hairs just under the lower jaw and fired again.

facing the wind to help hold the tent down. They started a Coleman stove in the first tent and pushed me in to get warm. It was an eight by ten canvas tent with double insulated walls. They covered the floor with caribou skins, then a large tarp, and finally our sleeping bags. After a few minutes I could remove my outer parka and still be comfortable. Soon my guide returned to check my face and said it was all right. One guide made dinner while the other skinned the musk ox that had been brought down to camp. Beef stew never tasted so good. After dinner the guides checked in on their radios. Included in their standard equipment are SBX 11 radios which allow them to talk to the base at Holman. Soon I was down to my regular clothes and quite comfortable. I got a short course in Eskimo. I remembered the stories from World War II when they used them to talk on radios so the Japanese could not understand the message. Sleep came easily.

The sound of a guide chipping ice from the floor for the morning's coffee awoke me. The tent had a heavy layer of dew on it but was still quite cozy. I started putting on layers of clothing and emerged from my sleeping bag. By this time eggs and ham were ready and the coffee tasted great. My first step outside reminded me of how cold it was. Tom and I kept warm walking around while the guides tore down camp. Within an hour the camp was on the sleds and we were ready to leave. The carcasses of the two musk oxen had frozen solid overnight but we captured the best strips of meat to take home.

We took a short cut over the ridges and headed straight for the sea. The going was slow at first but soon we were looking out over the frozen ocean. We slowly made our way down the steep embankment to an area away where the snow was quite even. Here the guides revved up the snowmobiles and headed for home. The trip took us about four hours.

We found the whole crew smiling when we arrived home. We learned Alan had killed a musk ox out of the same herd just before we spotted the three bulls. He got his skinned in time to return that evening in the dark. We had hunted three full days and had taken five musk oxen. That night we celebrated with a large feast. We told stories about the cold and how we didn't know how many nights we were going to

We had hunted three full days and had taken five musk oxen.
That night we celebrated with a large feast.

stay out. It all seemed so far from the confines of the warm
Arctic Char Inn. It did not take long to get sleepy with a full
stomach. A single bed never felt so good.

Next morning we got the tour of the town. We saw two
beautiful polar bears that some of the guides had taken. Each
settlement had a strict quota out of which they could allow a
few sport hunting permits. Although you could hunt musk ox
by snowmobile, polar bear could only be hunted by dog sled.
Dog teams were sometimes tied behind the guides' houses. We
purchased some white fox pelts which were very plentiful due
to the lack of predators. Some of the islands boasted big fox
populations. Holman is on a large bay which was frozen solid
but we noticed a lot of fishing boats along the bank. We
found out this was a major source of income in the summer
months, both for sport and commercial fishing. There were
some streams on the island that were supposed to be good
fishing for Arctic Char. Our guides had taken our skins to
their homes to thaw and have the women flesh them. Once
fleshed out they would be folded into a large fish box and put

Next morning we got the tour of the town. We saw two beautiful polar bears that some of the guides had taken.

outside where they would quickly freeze again.

That evening we went to a bingo party they arranged for us and met the rest of the town. The principal of the school was about our age and we had an interesting discussion about the system in place in the north. He said during his eight years at Holman, only one student had left to get a higher education—that of airplane mechanic. But when jobs got scarce the student returned to the island. We were surprised to learn many of the houses had television; a few even had computers. We went back to the Inn that night with renewed respect for these people of the north. Some of them had only moved to town within the last ten years.

The next morning we packed and then toured the school. The children had all sorts of questions about life in the United States. Then we went to the Coop where artisans were drawing on skins and carving on ivory. This provides a substantial part of their annual income. We went to the museum where we saw some of the early tools and weapons used in this harsh land. It was hard to imagine being out in a small boat chasing a whale with only a spear. The danger was mind boggling. The people were very proud of their heritage. The fact that they have survived when most societies would have failed was important to them. After lunch we loaded our gear in the pickup and headed for the airport. We said goodbye to the guides and boarded the King Air. After a smooth takeoff we headed out over the ice pack.

The ice pack looked foreboding from the air. Our thoughts and talk turned to the prospect of polar bear hunting on a dogsled. My nose and face were starting to peel from the brief exposure while taking pictures. I couldn't imagine two weeks on the icepack in a tent! Soon we landed at Paulatuk to pick up some passengers on their way to Inuvik. Paulatuk is a small town sitting on the mainland in Darniey Bay. When the passengers were in place we headed for Inuvik. Jessie was waiting with the van and soon we were at the motel. That night we met the hunters from Sachs Harbor and learned all had taken musk ox including one bow hunter. We celebrated with lobster and filet mignon—quite a feast two hundred and fifty miles above the Arctic Circle.

Jessie took us to the airport for the long flight home. We left at midnight arriving in Yellowknife for a brief stop in Edmonton at 2 A.M. We headed straight for the restaurant to have an early breakfast and take a nap. Our connecting flights started about 6 A.M. We also had to pass through customs with our hides and guns. Tom and Don headed east while Alan, Dion, and I headed south to Salt Lake City. Here after a short layover we were on our way home.

Flying over the mountains in a small plane brought back memories of the frozen tundra and of the small Inuits, who have made life in a very harsh environment. By now my nose had turned brown and the skin was really peeling to add character for the return home.

12

Baja California —
Last of the Four

As I mentioned before, getting a desert sheep permit is the hardest one to acquire. I had been applying in Nevada and Arizona for nine years without success. My friend Tom had killed a bighorn in British Columbia and now we both had three of the four sheep. We decided that if I could get two permits from Mexico we would try to finish our grand slam. My two friends who had been with the Game Department were no longer there, so Michael Valencia in Los Angeles arranged our hunts in Mexico. He made the necessary arrangements and confirmed the schedule. I chose to go to southern Baja; Tom was to hunt in the north. I scheduled my hunt at 'San Gregorio in the middle of Baja California and with the benefit of burros.

We met in Denver and flew to Tucson. There we separated, I flew to Hermosillo and Tom went on to Mexicali. The Aero Mexico flight to Hermosillo was just long enough to allow one to think of all the problems that could happen on a desert sheep hunt. Roberto Campo of the Department of Fish and Game met my flight. He rushed me through customs and took me to the beautiful Holiday Inn in Hermosillo. The efficiency of his manner bolstered my confidence in the hunt. The high rise was a delightful prehunt stay with a pool and other amenities. Roberto drove me to another motel to introduce four other hunters from Mexico who would go with me the following day.

The next morning, precisely at eleven, we cleared the guns and ammo with the military general. He *only* signs papers at eleven! This formality was to be adhered to even with all the prehunt paperwork. By one in the afternoon we were at the airport. We took pictures and loaded our gear into two twin engine planes for the flight to Bahia de Los Angeles. The flight took an hour and ten minutes. As we left the crowded urban area of Hermosillo, the landscape gave way to the large ranch-like areas of the southwest. It was very brown even for January. Next we came to the Bay of California, a lush blue compared to the surrounding land. We flew across the bay and over a large island in the middle called Cook Island. The terrain had changed to mountainous but still looked brown. The plane descended over a small fishing village and we were soon on the ground.

A van met us and took us to the Villa Vitto Hotel. We checked in and soon were sitting around the pool with a cold Mexican beer. One gentleman spoke excellent English and he told me there was a father and son on the hunt plus two men who had hunted extensively throughout Mexico. Two of the four had killed jaguar, an exotic of North American Game. Two hours later as it was getting dark, Francisco "Frankie" Aguilar arrived from the Fish and Game Department. He said he would be my guide. The supply truck from Mexicali hasn't arrived, and we might be here for a few days before our hunt could start; he told us. It disappointed everyone not to go right to camp. But we tried to make the most of it by having a great dinner and telling some old hunting stories.

The season in Mexico runs from late November to just before Christmas. Then it starts again around the end of January and runs until late March. We had picked the first hunt after Christmas break. I was beginning to think this may have been a mistake since the supplies still had not arrived. At noon the next day the Mexican hunters called Roberto in Hermosillo to see if they could get moving quicker. The little fishing village only had a radio phone, which was available a few hours each day. Soon we got a call back saying someone would be there in the morning to take me hunting. The others remained in limbo. We toured the town down to the water's edge and the few fishing boats there. That night over lobster Thomas and Luis told stories of their extensive hunting in Mexico.

Next morning Frankie showed up early for breakfast. I said goodbye to the other hunters, wished them good luck on their hunt, packed, and we got on the road. We drove to Puerto Puenta, a small village in the middle of Baja. We loaded supplies into a four wheel drive. Frankie picked up Cisco, another pair of eyes, and two boys to work the camp. We drove into the mountains toward the bay of California.

The roads were rough, the going slow. The valley floor had a few trees and greenery but everything else looked like desert.

After about four hours we came to beautiful mission in the middle of nowhere. It was called San Borco. We stopped, took some pictures, watered, and made an offering for a successful hunt. The land surrounding the mission looked like an oasis in the desert. A spring watered many trees and irrigated the garden which gave a lush feeling to the stark surroundings.

We traveled another few miles to the base of a large canyon and made camp. Over a campfire and a hot meal we discussed the next day's hunt. Not taking time to set up camp, we threw our sleeping bags on the ground and went to sleep. Next morning we started after an egg and Tang breakfast. We walked up a dry creek bed. It was full of rocks that were hard to maneuver on at the speed the guides had set. After a difficult climb to the top of a small hill, a vista of large basins opened in front of us. Here Frankie and Cisco found a comfortable spot to glass the surrounding basins. The basins were four to five miles away. It was difficult to concentrate on the desert caves. I had a pair of ten power Zeiss but both the guides were using twenty power Zeiss. I learned they had killed two rams in this area the previous March.

Descending to the valley floor we crossed a large open area to get to the base of the next canyon. At this point the temperature was about 100 degrees—and that's hot! We sat in the shade of a large cactus and glassed some more. We saw no sheep by 3 P.M., so decided to head for camp which was four or five miles away. Exhausted and hungry I was having trouble on the rocks again. I twisted my ankle badly and dropped my rifle. It hit hard. The next hour was a very painful walk to camp.

The cook had dinner ready when we arrived. I elevated my foot while I ate. With my strength renewed a little, I wrapped my ankle in an ace bandage and put on a higher boot. While Frankie and Cisco were putting up the tents, I resighted my rifle. At first I couldn't hit a twelve inch cactus at twenty five feet. It had been knocked badly out of sight. It always pays to bring extra ammo.

Sleeping in a tent was more comfortable than the night before. I still had to elevate my foot all night to help keep the swelling down. Although this was the fifth day of the hunt it had been my first day actually hunting. The sun seemed to have taken its toll. I felt exhausted. Not being able to sleep well didn't help. Next morning we packed early and moved about five miles north to another large basin. We didn't set up camp because the plan was to get to the main camp of San Gregorio that night. We set out for a set of hills about five miles away. Here again we found a comfortable seat and started glassing. After a few hours we moved to a spot where the canyon splits. We took the right side and found a good glassing spot. Cisco set up the spotting scope. I saw my first desert ram. It was laying on a rock outcropping with its head in the sun just like a picture. From this distance I couldn't judge it. The guides couldn't either.

The ram didn't look that big but Frankie wanted to get a closer look. We stalked to within five hundred yards and by this time my ankle was swollen and sore. The higher boots made the walking more comfortable but the last few hours had aggravated the swelling. Frankie and Cisco got a little closer but said the ram was only a three quarter curl that would score 150. After a short rest and discussion of the ram we headed back to the pickup and hopefully to the originally planned camp. The burros sounded like a great idea for my sore ankle. After a bruising ride, we reached San Gregorio. The camp still wasn't ready for hunters but soon the truck arrived with supplies. We had stopped at San Borco for water so we wouldn't be dehydrated by the time we made camp.

San Gregorio sits at the end of a narrow canyon with a cross high above the entrance. The cooking area was a shack with wooden and metal walls. The area also had some flat places with tents. As soon as the truck arrived they busied themselves putting up a comfortable tent. After a dinner of noodles and hot dogs I finally could store my gear and stand up to change clothes. Next I did a little exploring and found a spring at the base of the surrounding cliffs. A narrow but well used path wound up to a stone house that was once a beautiful hacienda. There were many stone corrals for the sheep and cattle. One can only wonder what these large ranches were like a hundred years ago. Everyone must have traveled to the church on Sunday by horses or cattle-drawn carts.

The next morning we sent the four wheel drive to Puerto Prieta for supplies while Frankie, Cisco, and I went hunting. We walked a long time on the canyon floor. Finally my ankle felt like it would be able to hold up under the stress of the hunt. After learning all the cactus names we climbed out of the valley to a large flat mesa. On the way up we jumped a mule deer doe and marveled at how fast she disappeared. On top we all found a shady spot and started to glass. Here I learned that a Mexican hunter had missed a very large ram about a month before. They had watched three groups of sheep before making the final stalk only to have the hunter miss. We could see a long distance—almost entirely around the mesa. We glassed from ten in the morning to two in the afternoon without seeing a sheep. By this time the temperature was broiling and we decided to make our way back to camp. At camp we had a meal of chicken soup and Tang.

The camp was situated so that by 3 P.M. the tents were in the shade and the temperature became more comfortable. After a short nap, a commotion outside my tent woke me up. Finally on the evening of the sixth day of the hunt the first load of supplies and one burro arrived. We got a second cook, supplies, a biologist, and one burro. One of the younger guides said that while watching cattle he had seen eight rams in an upper basin. Our spirits lifted knowing there were sheep in the area. That night I finally got a decent night's sleep. I kept thinking how tough this hunt really was in constant heat and sun. It became obvious we had been spike camping because the camp was not ready after the break.

Finally on the evening of the sixth day of the hunt
the first load of supplies and one burro arrived.

The next morning—with supplies replenished—breakfast consisted of steak, french fries, and a tossed salad. After packing for a few days, we headed up the intricate pathway without the benefit of the burro. The walk was all uphill at a gentle rate after the initial climb from the valley floor. The long narrow canyon wound up the path of a dry creek bed for six or seven miles. Finally we came to some cattle and soon found a running stream. The water came out of the ground, ran two hundred yards, then disappeared again. The upper camp consisted of some broken down buildings left from a time when mining and cattle were active in the area. We had walked continuously since eight in the morning and it was now eleven. The sun was high and hot. We took off our packs and sat down in the shade to cool off and have lunch.

We had a light lunch and the guides started to glass the surrounding valley walls. After an hour or so as I was dozing off, the guides excitedly called me to look through the spotting scope. To my amazement about two miles away slowly making their way down a steep slope was a band of seven sheep. Everything moves slow in this hot country, even the coyotes we ran into were lethargic. They just walked at a pace where they would not burn any extra energy. After a long study, we could make out three rams and two ewes for sure. They were still a long way off but two of the rams looked mature. The mountain in front of us was steep and high, probably three thousand feet from the valley floor to the top. There were scree rock slides mixed with steep ridges running straight up to the top. Yet we had to approach them from above if possible. We had a conference and decided it was now or never.

We backtracked about a hundred yards to get out of sight and found a dry creek bed running out of the mountain to hide our movement. We headed into the ravine for a few hundred yards then straight up until we were under the steepest part of the mountain. This took about an hour and a half in the hottest part of the day. Here we started slowly across the scree rock slides toward where we last saw the sheep. We continued to work toward the sheep hoping they had moved under us. My feet were sore and my ankle hurt like hell. I had to stop and rest frequently. Finally when we thought we would be right above the sheep we crept down to the edge of the rim hoping to spot them. As we looked over we were disappointed. We saw nothing. We had just spent three hours climbing to the edge of the basin where we had seen the sheep—only to have them disappear.

Francisco and one of the younger guides headed back to make sure they had not worked under and behind us. Cisco went ahead to check the next basin. I crept along with a young Mexican to make sure I did not have an accident. As I looked up I saw Cisco waving us forward. After a scary scramble across the scree rock, I was about thirty yards from a ridge-like area which shielded the next basin. I looked up to see Cisco and Frankie glassing the basin. Cisco was about thirty yards above Frankie and was waving frantically. I put a shell in the chamber and hobbled as fast as I could up the hill.

When I reached the top of the rock pile I could see seven sheep running straight away from me about two hundred yards away. Cisco told me the largest ram was in the back and that I should take him. I rested the gun on the rock but could see only white butts in the scope. When they reached the next rock crest they had to turn to go down to avoid going over the cliff. They bunched up and the last ram had to wait for the other rams to clear out in front of him. As he turned to go down I had a broadside shot and placed the crosshairs low on the front shoulder and squeezed the trigger. He staggered to the left. I could only see his white butt, then he disappeared. Frankie started yelling and jumping up and down with joy. Cisco and I could not see anything because the sheep were out of our sight.

This whole event took all of ten seconds from the moment Cisco started waving. If I would have had to chamber a bullet I would never have got the shot off. Finally Frankie yelled to Cisco who translated for me that the ram had fallen off a small cliff and became wedged against a bush. I was ecstatic. I scrambled across the next basin to search for my reward. At the bottom of the small cliff laid the magnificent animal. I looked down on the last of the four of my North American Grand Slam. After congratulations between the five of us, we decided it was too late to get the ram off the mountain. It was 5 P.M. and getting dark. We cleaned the animal and placed him in a large bush so he had no chance of rolling down the mountainside. Our legs were tired and we slowly made our way to the valley floor to meet the two young guides who were carrying Frankie and Cisco's packs. More congratulations and we were on a good path in the bottom of the valley floor.

We had walked a total of about fourteen miles. Every step was agony.

I looked down on the last of the four of my North American Grand Slam. My weariness could not subdue my feeling of accomplishment at completing my Grand Slam!

This feeling overwhelmed me on the slow, tough walk back to camp. It seemed like it never really happened. It was almost dark when we reached the upper camp. We made a light dinner of tuna, tortillas, corn, lettuce, and some Tang. Two hours after we had climbed into the sleeping bags the burros arrived. These were the same burros we expected to be here six days ago to help with the hunt. I slept fitfully that night because of the anticipation of the next day. I wondered how Tom was doing five hundred miles to the north. Little did I know he was back in Indianapolis. He'd had a hair raising hunt, wounding a large ram and tracking it for twenty four hours straight before making the kill.

We were up early the next morning, had a breakfast of Tang, and headed up the dry creek bed toward the ram. This time we took two burros, one to carry the sheep and the other for me to ride if I got tired. We arrived just as the sun came over the hill. We made our way underneath the sheep, then climbed four hundred yards straight up to where we had left him. I took bunches of pictures. With a rope around the horns Frankie and a young guide slowly lowered the ram down to an area where the other guide had brought the burros. After loading the burro with the sheep we made our way down to the valley floor and back to the mining camp.

Frankie at the upper camp.

The biologist who had all his tapes and papers ready met us at the mining camp. He measured the horns at 37 inches long with 16½ inch bases. He then measured length, height, body cavity sizes, and weight. He pulled a tooth for aging and looked at the general health of the animal. The ram was fat and seemed in good shape. It was now midmorning and we loaded the ram on a burro and in a *dead heat walk* made it back to San Gregorio in about three hours. The going is much easier down hill on a good path and the trip seemed much shorter. The pack string arrived an hour and a half later.

After caping the head and salting the hide, we immediately headed for Bahia de Los Angeles. I was already in the tent thinking about a good night's sleep. Instead we hit the bumpy road back to San Borco and then on to Bahia de Los Angeles for a celebration. After about five hours we hit the asphalt road. We were only twenty minutes from the Villa Vitto Hotel. We arrived at 7 P.M. and had a celebration dinner. Two hours later the guides headed for Puerto Prieta and I hit the shower.

We loaded the ram on a burro and made it back to San Gregorio in about three hours. The pack string arrived an hour and a half later.

Next morning I resalted the cape in the bathtub and waited by the pool. After lunch a two engine plane circled and landed. To this day, I don't know how Roberto found out the hunt was over. I quickly packed my gear and after the short van ride to the airport, loaded the plane and we were off to Hermosillo.

Roberto was waiting and was very proud of the sheep. We exchanged stories of the other hunters I met prior to the hunt. He took me to the motel and I soaked up some Mexican sun and beer. He arrived with his sons and we all went to dinner.

Next day I got the official tour of the Fish and Game Office prior to my Aero Mexico flight to Tucson. I said goodbye sadly after nine days of the toughest hunting I have ever encountered. Customs in Tucson was relatively easy with Roberto's paper work. Then I was off to Denver and home.

13

Boone and Crockett Antelope

One of the niceties of living in Colorado is the abundance of wildlife. As a resident you can occasionally draw a permit that allows you to take a special animal. Such a permit came my way in 1986 as an antelope tag in A301. I had already taken a very respectable antelope on a hunt in Lusk, Wyoming. One of my first trophies was an antelope taken at Douglas, Wyoming with my dad in 1972. It was my first trip through Wyoming and I was impressed by the abundance of these animals along the roads between Afton and Douglas. My second trip to the southeast corner of Wyoming proved there were even more antelope from Cheyenne to Lusk.

Most antelope in Colorado are located in the northwest corner around Craig in the areas A1, A2, A3, and A301. In fewer numbers, they range east of Denver in what we would call the plains of Colorado. After drawing the permit I contacted Dion Luke of Ragged Mountain Outfitters who, as a youngster, spent his summers on a ranch around Craig. I knew A301 was in his area. He had also drawn a tag for the area. We decided to spend one of the last weekends in September hunting antelope.

The pronghorn is one of the great conservation comebacks in North America. In the early 1800s the estimated population was in the vicinity of 40 million. Their numbers bottomed out in the 1920s at only about 13,000. Due to conservation, good game management, and enforcement of laws we now have more than 800,000 pronghorn in North America. Four hundred thousand of these reside in Wyoming. Pronghorns range from the southern plains of Saskatchewan in Alberta, down through the center of North Dakota, South Dakota, Nebraska, western Kansas, Oklahoma, Texas, and spill over into old Mexico. The western borders are Arizona, Nevada, eastern California, Oregon, and Washington. They are in abundance in all the mountain states in between.

The pronghorn isn't actually an antelope; it is not related to any of the true antelope family of Africa. It is considered a type of goat. It has the unique distinction of being the only hoofed mammal in the world that sheds the outer portion of its horn every year. It never sheds the core of the horn. The outside is cast off by a new horn sheath that forms underneath. The new growth starts at the very tip of the horn core and grows downward. The cast is separated from the core by a layer of tissue.

Ordinarily the horns project up and slightly forward with the prongs projecting either forward or upward. There is much variation in the shape of the horns; some project forward, some grow back, some hook forward, and some bend out sideways. Accidents have produced records of many odd heads with horns broken, bent, and regrown in just about every imaginable position.

The large male pronghorn is about the size of a whitetail deer standing—36-42 inches high at the shoulder. He, however, has a chunkier body. A pronghorn buck measures about five feet in length and weighs 100-140 pounds. The does are smaller, seldom weighing 100 pounds. The male and female are marked alike except for the male's broad black *chin strap* extending between the ears and the throat.

The pronghorn also has the distinction of being the only hoofed mammal in North America, having only two toes on each foot. It is the fastest running land animal in North America. Its speed of 55 mph is exceeded only by the cheetah's short bursts of speed of about 70 mph. The pronghorn can sustain speeds of 35-40 mph for long distances. The terrain to which the animal adapts has produced a runner, not a jumper. There is a measured horizontal jump of 27 feet, but the pronghorn can't jump high. It just never developed that skill. Living on the flat open prairies, these flat footed animals needed a good horizontal jump to clear ditches and gullies. There was nothing to jump over until man put up fences.

Sagebrush is the primary food when it can be found. Much of the pronghorn's comeback has been fostered inadvertently by cattle overgrazing. Sagebrush is now the dominant plant on what was once grassland in the time of the buffalo. Ranches who run more cattle than the land will support have a situation where the cattle eat all the grasses. This encourages growth of sagebrush. In each succeeding decade the land will support less and less cattle as more and more acres are overrun by sagebrush. Snowberry, rabbit brush, and salt brush are also major foods for the pronghorn.

Dominant bucks have territories that they defend from early spring to late fall. Each buck will gather as many does, with their accompanying fawns and yearlings, as he can control. This ranges from 5-15 adult does. The breeding season usually occurs the last part of August through September. The gestation period is approximately 250 days. A doe giving birth for the first time usually has a single fawn; thereafter she normally has twins.

The coyote is their major predator since its range coincides exactly with that of the pronghorn. Although coyotes feed mainly on fawns or unhealthy adults, occasionally a group of coyotes will run an adult in a circle and—by running relays—tire the pronghorn and kill it. The bobcat is also a major predator. Deep snow is the pronghorn's deadliest natural enemy.

For our antelope hunt we decided to drive to Craig, which is about 1½ hours north of Glenwood Springs and spend the night. We got there in the early afternoon and made our way out to one of the ranches we wanted to look at. We did some scouting by glassing in the evening and saw many groups of antelope with dominant bucks being in almost full rut. Each buck was continually chasing the does to try to keep them from moving away from his area. If the weather held, we figured we would have an excellent chance of taking a trophy-quality buck.

We left the motel the next morning while it was still dark and headed north through the sagebrush country of north-western Colorado. After a cup of coffee at the rancher's house, we went to find our first group of antelope. A short drive later we parked the truck and walked up over a hill. About a mile in the distance we could see an antelope buck chasing 15 does in his continuing attempt to maintain his harem. They were feeding in a cut wheat field and back into the sagebrush. We set up the spotting scope and glassed the animal.

As light approached from the east, we decided to stalk. We jumped over the hill and made our way down through a long gully out of his sight. Here we could cover about 1000 yards of the mile to get within range of the antelope. They were slowly feeding up a long gully; we figured if we made our way toward the head of the gully we could cut them off. When we reached the end of the gully we climbed over a small hump and waited for the herd. The wind was blowing in our face so we knew if we were quiet this stalk would be easy. The antelope were slowly approaching, but were still 200 yards away. When they were within 150 yards the buck, still chasing the does and trying to keep them in a tight circle, made his way out to one side. This was my opening for a quick shot. One shot from my 30.06 put him down for good.

The does wandered away but stayed close enough to watch. We went over to the buck. He was truly a trophy. The horns measured 16¼ and he was heavy. We dragged him to the nearest place we could get the truck to, and loaded up.

Then we went to work getting an antelope for Dion. We drove for a few hours and looked over some respectable bucks. We decided to try a long stalk around a buck we saw lying along a small creek bed. I stayed on the ridge and glassed while Dion made a circular drive with the truck. Then he got out and stalked close to the buck antelope. The antelope jumped up and took off, but Dion nailed it with one shot. We drug the buck again to a spot we could drive to, and loaded him into the truck. The horns were somewhat smaller than my buck but he was still a trophy. We made our way back to the ranch house to cape and clean the animals.

The final measurement of my antelope scored 86⅝; after drying and deductions it scored 82⅜ points. This made the Boone and Crockett minimum *so I had one for the book.*

14

American Deer Slam

Colorado

During my first trip to Glenwood Springs in 1973 I took a young meat buck on the last day of the season. The next year I moved to Glenwood Springs in July and began scouting the surrounding areas for the mule deer season. I was just starting my practice and had little time, but when I could sneak away I spent my time in the foothills around Glenwood. Soon I was familiar with the surrounding terrain and noted that walking out of a canyon or river bottom took herculean effort. What might start out like an innocent hike would turn into a sweaty ordeal. Distances were deceiving and the altitude made it hard.

I had no access to horses and my only mode of transportation was by four wheel drive and foot. The Division of Wildlife during these years had eliminated the two deer limit and the seasons changed almost every year. Some years elk was first, followed by deer, and ended with a combined season. I also learned the weather was a major factor in game movement. Some years it would be dry and hot; other years cold with deep, heavy snows.

I soon met an avid hunter and farm real estate salesman who loved to hunt mule deer. We hit it off and he decided to show me some of his hot spots. He had access to farms he had listed for sale. I had killed a deer almost every year. But I still did not have a trophy four point western-count buck. He was determined I get one. We decided to hunt the early deer season so we could move around better. Don knew a sheep farmer who would let us on his property in Glenwood Canyon. The climb would be steep but once out of the canyon we'd be in prime deer habitat.

It was still dark when we passed French Creek. We drove about two miles east to Golden Bair's ranch, parked, and started walking to the north through a cedar covered hillside. It was cold but soon the sun came up and brought warmth. As soon as we went over the first bench, we started seeing deer. Does, fawns, and a few small bucks were everywhere. We came to a spot where we could look into a canyon on the east and an open field to the north and west. Don was going to work the ridge line and I would cross the field to a second ridge toward French Creek.

We walked together a little way, then parted wishing each other luck. I climbed to the ridge and found a cedar tree to sit under and glass. I had just sat down when I heard a noise behind me. I spotted a deer running through the scrub oak above me. I could see horns and took the safety off my gun. I couldn't get a good look at him through the scope. Finally he broke out of the bottom and stopped in a small grassy opening to feed. He was a good buck. I put the cross hairs behind his front shoulder and had my first trophy mule deer. The horns were heavy and a four by five western count with brow tines.

I cleaned him and waited. I couldn't figure out why Don hadn't shown up to help drag him out. Later I learned the ridges between Don and I had muffled the sound of the shot. He hadn't heard anything. I realized I couldn't drag it out by myself, so I decided to cut it in half and carry it. I brought both halves over the first ridge and left the back half on the trail while I carried the front half back to the vehicle.

The deer had come from Don's direction and I'm sure he had flushed it out of the thick scrub oak without hearing or seeing it. This is a good way for two hunters to approach an area so one has a chance of moving the deer to the other. I learned a lot about spotting game and the movement of game

**I had my first trophy mule deer. The horns were heavy—
a four by five western count with brow tines.**

from this first trophy. We had seen twenty to fifty deer a day mostly in the early light or late evening. I also found that moving slowly during the midday, one could find deer.

The next year we hunted some high basins behind Redstone, Colorado. Here above the timberline one could see the ridges and basins were alive with hunters. We had horses this year but the weather was hot and dry and the bucks were no where to be found. The altitude was ten to twelve thousand feet and the scenery magnificent.

The next year we obtained access to a lower ranch through one of my patients who was also listed with Don. Spring Valley was a plateau two thousand feet above Glenwood Springs. The game wintered there to get away from the deep snows. Don brought his son along. Destry was out to kill his first deer. We worked the aspen thickets to no avail during the last season. It had snowed a fair amount but was warm enough to have melted in many places.

The farm we were hunting had dry land wheat farming mixed with heavy scrub oak thickets and sagebrush flats. Since it was only twenty minutes from Glenwood we hunted the weekends and after work. The last day we had just left a wheat stubble field on our way to a sagebrush flat when Don noticed a buck with a few does. A road divided the property and we didn't think the deer would cross it so we devised a scheme to get Destry a shot. I took Destry toward a point where we hoped we could see the deer as they came toward the road. Don tried to push them toward us.

It worked great. After about ten minutes I saw the first doe. I told Destry to get ready as four more does passed. The buck came slowly with this head down. He was in full rut. I told Destry to take his time and he pulled the trigger. It was a clean miss and I told him to reload. He raised his gun but the deer started to run. When he pulled the trigger all I heard was a click. He had ejected a casing but had not thrust a new shell into the chamber. The buck was about to disappear and Destry wasn't near ready. I pulled up, led the deer to the left, and squeezed. The buck dropped in his tracks.

The deer was bigger than the one I had killed two years before.

Don and Destry took off to see if they could find another buck before it got dark. I set about the task of cleaning the animal and getting him to the truck.

The next year Destry got his first buck on the same ranch!

Santa Barbara Deer

My quest for the four species of deer—which turned out to be five—began in earnest in September of 1985. I had already taken whitetail deer in Pennsylvania. And I had three mature mule deer killed in Garfield County, Colorado. To get started on the other species, I contacted Alan Baier. He had a hunt advertised for coastal blacktail north of Santa Barbara, California. Tom Phillippe, Jr., my hunting companion on the desert sheep hunt and previous hunt in musk ox country, decided to join me on these upcoming deer hunts.

Alan met us at the Santa Barbara airport. A three hour drive took us north through Santa Maria and San Luis Obispo to Paso Robles. We turned and headed toward the coast on Highway 46, soon finding ourselves turning at a large cattle ranch. The terrain was very interesting. As we drove we noticed dry underbrush with green hillsides due to the type of trees in the area. It looked a lot like some of the hilly areas in Africa that I had visited.

After we checked into our bunks we headed out for a four wheel drive tour of the ranch. It was late afternoon by this time and we saw lots of deer, although no trophy bucks were present. Alan had one previous hunt here when he had taken two good bucks. From what we could see these deer were like whitetail deer as to their habitat and in their movement. We settled down that night and talked about our previous hunting experiences around the warm glow of the fire at the lodge.

The next morning we were up early and back on the four wheel drive trails. We traversed the ranch to find only does and fawns. We decided to do some drives along ridges of this covered hillside. Alan took Tommy down to the end of one small canyon, then came back and drove the side of the hillside chasing out a few deer, but nothing with any horn size. The ones we saw were smaller in size and quite gray looking.

Although this ranch was only a few miles from a busy freeway, it felt like we were in a far removed land. We saw or heard no vehicles or other people. The privacy of the large cattle ranch was astonishing. A large bobcat loped by, and later another. We also saw some wild boar as well as the many breeds of cattle that were raised here.

After lunch we headed out. Coming over the first hill we noticed a small group of deer with a three point buck. After a short stalk, Tommy had it on the ground. He was quite happy with his third species of deer. The deer in the area have tall horns and a large Y buck was a very good trophy. They also have long brow tines to go along with the Y, which make them look like a spectacularly long three point. This was the case in Tommy's deer. We loaded it and headed back to the ranch to celebrate.

After hanging the deer, Alan took me out to an area where there was thick cover. We watched a canyon on one side and a large meadow sprinkled with hardwood trees. I was making my way slowly through the hardwood trees toward the brushier hillside when up jumped the largest deer we had seen. My shot knocked it down but it jumped right back up and ran along the ridge. I scrambled to the top of the ridge and fired another shot as the deer ran straight away from me. It disappeared into the heavy cover.

The chase was on. It was quickly getting dark and after finding blood we hurried our stalk through a steep canyon and back along the ridge. After going along the ridge for about 300 yards we found the deer bedded down. One shot finished it off. We celebrated that night with two trophies from a short 2½ day hunt.

The following morning we were out again looking for further trophies but saw none along the dry hillsides. We did see another bobcat during this period. By mid afternoon we'd decided to hang it up and catch our plane back to Colorado−two very successful hunters.

We celebrated that night with two trophies from a short 2½ day hunt.

Geronimo's Trail

The following November I took a nice whitetail in the Tamarack area around Sterling, Colorado. We met with Gary VonSchmidt who had been a hunting guide for Alan Baier. He was doing most of the Coues deer hunting in southern New Mexico. We discussed the hunt and decided it would be worth the try to complete our American deer slam. There was no drawing for permits and we only had to purchase a New Mexico deer license so we set out at the end of November for a week's hunt in the southern tip of New Mexico.

After leaving Glenwood Springs at 4 o'clock in the afternoon our first night found us in Taos, New Mexico. The next morning we were up early and heading south through Santa Fe and Albuquerque. After a long drive we arrived at Animas, New Mexico—about 45 miles north of the Mexican border at 5:00 in the afternoon. Our guide, Gary VonSchmidt, met us. He had some bad luck with the transmission of his truck so my Chevy S-10 would come in handy.

Geronimo Trail Camp

We loaded my truck and headed south from Animas on a dirt road to where we could see the Mexican border. Here the Geronimo Trail heads straight west into Arizona through the Coronado National Forest. This is where we would hunt. It was interesting to see the spacious New Mexico flatland turn into a wooded pine forest. After a short drive we came to a stream where we set up the tent camp. Gary had brought a friend, John, who was to be the camp tender.

It had rained very hard that day, which was very unusual for this time of year. We found out later it made hunting much more difficult. The deer, who usually moved due to lack of water, stopped moving because the rain had filled many of the small pools which were usually empty.

Up early the next morning, we climbed a small ridge just south of our camp where Gary had seen a six point Coues. After climbing about half an hour, we were only 600-800 feet off the craggy floor. We noticed the rocky dry ground was similar to the desert sheep hunt we had been on eleven months before. When we reached the first small range south of camp, Gary and Tommy made a circular drive and found a six point buck. He ran by with amazing speed. He was much smaller than I had expected. I could have probably gotten a shot, but I thought his horns were a bit small for this early in the hunt. Later I was to find out he was actually a good buck.

We walked many miles that day making a sweep to the south and west almost to the Mexican border, and finding several feral pigs at one small water hole. This wilderness was interesting. We saw many does but no more bucks the rest of the day. We headed back to camp tired and ready for the evening meal.

The next day we headed west on the Geronimo Trail to a point a few miles east of the Arizona state line. Here we climbed a high plateau and immediately noticed the difference. Although quite rocky, there were grassy areas between scrub groves that were excellent deer country. We found the skeleton of a beautiful eight point Coues wrapped in fence wire. The carcass had been stripped by a bear or coyotes. Although the country looked lush we made some heavy drives through the thick brush and saw but one small buck. He only gave us a glimpse and minimal time to shoot. We circled the canyons from atop the high plateau many times that day and didn't see another buck.

For the next three days we hunted this high plateau and lush area. The next day we worked the top of the plateau until mid afternoon and again saw only one small buck. The long climb down exhausted us. We spent the evening going south or north of camp to do some heavy scouting with our glasses. As usual there were many does and fawns but no shootable bucks.

The next day we saw Coatimundi and seven Goul's turkeys with their silver and black feathers. We felt we were working very hard each day. But we were having no luck on trophy quality bucks, in fact we were seeing very few deer. There weren't many hunters in the area. We weren't sure whether it was the lack of hunters or the abundance of rain that had made the hunting hard.

The fifth day we were up bright and early. Again we headed for the high plateau. We made a circular stalk and only kicked out the one small buck we had seen the previous day. Finally at lunch Gary and I decided that the pressure from working the tops possibly could have driven the deer down along the sides. There was a long steep ridge which worked along the side of the road that ran into Arizona. We felt if we went down this ridge into some steep canyons and left Tommy on top that anything we kicked out might run uphill toward him. It was about a 60 degree angle with many rocks and cactus.

We had to move very slowly underneath the ridge. Gary was about 100 yards below me and continued along the bottom. We hoped anything he jumped would run uphill. We had worked our way back about three miles and were quite close to where we had parked the truck when we came upon one of the last small canyons. I stepped across the canyon and spun around to look at a crash sound behind me. Two Coues bucks jumped up. The largest ran straight toward me. I pulled the trigger but nothing happened. The buck veered five feet from me and ran straight uphill. By the time I realized that the safety was on, moved it forward, and took a fleeting shot—I'd missed him. The second Coues had no escape route. He ran up the hill but was still in sight. One shot put him on the ground and I had my deer slam.

The second Coues had no escape route. He ran up the hill but was still in sight. One shot put him on the ground and I had my deer slam.

When I walked up the hill, I couldn't believe my eyes. One side had five points. The other was only a spike plus three small points. Although totaling nine points, it was not a symmetrical rack. At this point in the hunt, however, I was ecstatic with the completion of my North American deer slam. Although walking the ridge, Tommy had not seen the large trophy buck come out on top. We rejoiced that night by going to Lordsburg for a good steak dinner.

The next day we headed back to the same spot and found the big ridge to the east. We placed Tommy on it so he could see any movement through a long canyon which we walked. We brought John along so we could make a nice slow drive hoping to push the larger buck up to Tommy. We walked slowly covering approximately 100 yards of the valley floor and finally started seeing deer activity although we couldn't make out any bucks.

All at once Tommy spotted a large Y buck who stood up and watched the three of us walk fairly close to him, then laid back down. Tommy worked his way down the ridge line and fired approximately 50 yards above the buck, killing him in his bed. The Y buck had heavy horns and a nice brow tines. He was a true trophy. I carried the deer out on my back. I couldn't believe how much this small deer weighed. We had worked very hard for six days and only found two deer to stalk and take. There was a tremendous effort put out to find the trophy Coues deer of the Southwest.

I drove Tommy back to Albuquerque that night where I put him on a plane for Indianapolis. After staying overnight, I returned to Glenwood Springs. Both of us now had a blacktail, mule deer, whitetail, and Coues whitetail deer. This completed our North American deer slam.

15

Continuing the Quest for North American Deer

A Floating Hunting Camp

The next year Tommy and I decided to continue our quest for deer. We booked a hunt for Sitka blacktail deer on Kodiak Island. We were to hunt from a large boat on Kodiak Island. I decided my dad, who is 70 years old, would love this type of trip. We also had applied for Nebraska whitetail licenses and had booked the hunt so that when we returned to Denver Tommy could go to Nebraska and hunt whitetail with Gary VonSchmidt. I would return home for a few days before going on to Nebraska.

Although there were many boats to hunt from, the Pacific Star kept coming to the forefront as *the boat* for this hunt. Managed by Quest Charters of Anchorage, Alaska, The Pacific Star is a 70 foot cabin cruiser used for sightseeing, whale watching, fishing, and viewing of the glaciers during the summer. Then it becomes a floating hunting camp in the fall. Quest Charters has hunts for brown bear, moose, and Sitka blacktail deer. The boat accommodates eight hunters. It's equipped for everyone's needs.

We had set the dates for November 7-14 at the previous year's Safari Club International convention. As November neared we became very excited knowing that we were going to return to some wild country. Although it had a lot of wet, rainy, sleety type of weather—no matter how hard the days were we could return to the warm shelter and excellent food of the cruiser at night. This self-guided hunt exceeded all expectations of anything we dreamed of. I flew from Denver, my dad from Pittsburgh, and Tommy from Indianapolis. We met in Chicago and flew to Anchorage. After spending the night in Anchorage, we continued on Mark Air to Kodiak. Ed Ward, captain of the Pacific Star, met us.

A short ride from the airport to the boat dock revealed a beautiful 70 foot cabin cruiser with all the amenities of home.

The accommodations on board consisted of two hunters per room, each having a bunk, and a place to store your clothes. They stored gun cases below. We received a short explanation of the boat activities and headed out on an eight hour trip around Kodiak Island to Uyak Bay, on the southwest corner of the island. We pulled into the bay at about 4 o'clock that afternoon after leaving Kodiak at 10 o'clock that morning. The country was quite brown; fall had taken full effect. There was snow on the top 500-800 feet of the mountains. Kodiak Island looked brown and grassy down to the beaches under the snow. There had not been enough snow to knock the grass down. It was still quite high.

Anticipating a cold and wet morning, we had a wonderful steak dinner cooked on a barbecue and went to our bunks early. The boat was equipped with generators and VCRs as well as books and leisurely meals in a warm atmosphere. The other members of the hunt included two from California and four from Alaska, for a total of nine. The crew consisted of Captain Ed Ward, skiff operator Cliff, chef Rick, and boat deck hand Daniel. These gentlemen were of great help throughout the trip. That night they explained what we needed to take with us, the use of a space blanket, and how to signal the boat for help if needed.

After a hearty breakfast, the skiff was ready at 7:30 to take us to the beach. It didn't get light until 8 o'clock and by then we were on the beach. The beaches consisted of very small areas approximate 50-100 yards long between cliff-like out croppings. The terrain was bench-like, steep and covered with alders as well as small open grassy plains. After walking about 1,000 feet off the beach it was obvious we would see many deer. We ran into three bucks with some does the first morning. My dad took a large Y buck and I took a three point. We weren't quite sure what size the horns were, but since you could shoot up to five deer we figured this was an excellent start.

We dragged them down to the beach by 2 o'clock in the afternoon and were picked up by Cliff in the skiff by 3:30. We carried the deer back to the Pacific Star where they were skinned, caped, and cut up by the crew. The meat was packaged in waxed boxes and could be shipped anywhere in the lower 48 states. Capes and horns are kept together and sent separately in other boxes. We found out we had taken two of the smaller bucks of the day. Other hunters had taken larger deer.

The boat moves at night and anchors in another portion of the bay which allows the skiff to move up and down this long bay for hunting. The next day they took us to an old mining site and left us on the beach. We climbed through the benches until we found a grassy meadow with a stream running out of it. A Y buck showed up on the side of the grassy meadow but we decided after seeing some of the larger bucks on the ship he was too small. I started down the stream and left my dad in the open meadow where he could see easily.

After walking 50 yards I saw three deer working up along the right side of the edge of the thicket. Going through the alders was tough; it was hard to get a good look at them. I noticed, however, one had good horns. They were heading straight toward my dad and I knew if I was very quiet they wouldn't spook. Likely he would get a shot. There were two bucks and one doe. I waited five minutes and heard the shot. I ran back to where dad had taken a very heavy 4 X 3 Sitka deer. He said they had come to the edge of the grassy area. The doe took the lead followed by the smaller buck and then the larger buck. The deer was quite stocky with beautiful coloring and made an excellent trophy which would later score in the gold medal class for my dad. I drug it down to the beach and dad returned to the boat. I continued to hunt without success.

I waited for an opening and put it on the ground.
It was a very heavy three point.

Tommy had picked up two three pointers which were quite heavy. The next day I went back to the burned out cannery and started to work up toward the small meadow where my dad had shot his deer. Once again light was coming on the meadow early in the morning and I saw the Y buck I'd seen before. After about an hour I slowly worked down the stream toward the beach. The alders got thicker and I noticed two deer moving slowly across the front of me to the alders on the left. One was a very heavy three point following a doe. I waited for an opening and put it on the ground. It was a very heavy three point. I got it down to the beach and to the boat. That night we all had respectable Sitka blacktails and the celebration started. After floating by Munsey's brown bear camp, famous on Kodiak Island, we moved one bay north heading back toward Kodiak.

The next day Tommy and I put out on an island between two bays. We worked ourselves up the side. Coming across the bottom was an asymmetrical four point Sitka blacktail. He hesitated in an opening just a second too long and I had my third blacktail. I drug him down to the beach and then headed to the top of the island. About two-thirds of the way up we broke out of the wooded hillsides and were on grassy plains. Here the brown bear tracks were thick along each trail. We worked up to the top of the island where we could see the Pacific Star settled in the middle of the bay a few thousand feet below. What a sight! After slowly working our way back to camp we saw many deer but no bucks that were larger than the ones we already had taken. The next day we moved camp out to the edge of the bay. Here Tommy and I again went on the beach and saw a very respectable four point but didn't get a shot at it. We returned that night happy and tired.

The other members of the party took 26 deer so our boat total was 33 for 5½ days. There were no brown bear encounters during this hunt. Two members who were hunting together saw a nine foot sow with a cub but did not bother it. Fresh bear tracks were seen in the snow by several others, but this was not to be a problem. Since the hills were so steep around the edges of the island one could always keep the Pacific Star in sight so you never felt you were too far from camp.

Although the hunting was very hard during the day you could return when tired as the skiff picked up hunters three times a day. Returning to the Pacific Star, clothes and boots could dry out. The availability of a hot shower and warm meal made this an excellent camp. Although quite clear the next day, we were unable to leave the bay because of the size of the waves in the open water. We turned back to the bay and spent an extra night before making it into Kodiak one day late.

We flew to Anchorage. My dad had a short time to catch his connection to Pittsburgh. Tommy and I didn't get off until 1:00 in the morning.

Platte Valley Bucks

Back in Denver, Tommy rented a car and headed east to Sterling where he met Gary VonSchmidt for the whitetail deer hunt. I went home to work for three days before joining them in Nebraska. John Johnson was in Sterling, Colorado and joined Tommy for the two hour drive from Sterling to the Platte River in Nebraska. By Wednesday John was home with a nice ten point whitetail buck. Tommy had also connected on a ten point buck. He was to spend Wednesday night in Denver prior to catching a plane to Indianapolis Thursday morning. I drove over from Glenwood Springs to join him. I would be driving to Nebraska on Thursday morning to start the hunt.

Tommy and John had been met by a strong snowstorm that had blown through Denver and provided excellent hunting conditions in Nebraska and eastern Colorado during the first weekend. Hunting took place mainly from tree stands and along the edge of a lot of wheat and corn fields and the 10-12 inches of snow that blanketed the area provided excellent cover as well as a perfect source of fresh tracking for whitetail. The snowstorm had tailed off by the time I drove to Denver.

After seeing Tommy's horns I anxiously looked forward to my trip to Nebraska. I had already killed an eight and nine point whitetail along the Tamarack area just east of Sterling, Colorado. I put Tommy on the plane and headed to Sterling where I met Gary at noon on Thursday. We drove the two hours north to the Platte River area of Nebraska and met the rancher where we were to hunt.

Having had John and Tommy there the previous weekend, he decided an area with heaviest cover along the river would provide the best bet for a deer. That night we drove out into the wheat fields of melting snow and saw a small buck and a doe. The next morning we were at the edge of the hayfield. We waited for the deer in the middle of the field to come toward the river bottom. We saw a 10 point buck 300-400 yards away but were unable to close in for a shot. We made our way to the river bottom and got into the tree stand. I spent the rest of the morning in the tree stand seeing a few deer crossing a small slough 250-300 yards behind me. The

I decided to get out of the tree stand and work up to an area
where there was a clump of grass that formed a small blind
in front of the slough.

cattails had been worked very heavily by the whitetail deer and trails traversing them were easy to see in the fresh snow. I discovered most of the deer were crossing the slough 300 yards east of me over to a small island. As dark approached the geese came back to the river. It was quite a sight.

Next morning we had breakfast at Lake McConnahy. We were back at the edge of the field before daybreak. Once again we noticed a small amount of deer in the field but to our right we also heard some bugling type noises. We were amazed as light came to the field to see a large five point bull elk and a smaller elk facing off at the edge of the field. By 20 minutes after light they had worked their way into the river bottom and disappeared. Who ever heard of elk in Nebraska? I headed for the tree stand I was in before and stayed there most of the morning. I saw a few small does but no buck worth shooting.

The slough behind me still seemed to have most of the activity. I returned to the stand at about 3 P.M. and noticed the deer were again crossing onto the small island. I decided to get out of the tree stand and work up to an area where there was a clump of grass that formed a small blind in front of the slough. It was almost dark when a doe came out on the other side. She disappeared into the heavy growth at the side of the stream just as the geese started coming over.

I waited a few more minutes and a large buck came out of the willows and started across the slough. I couldn't see his horns until he caught the scent of the doe and followed her track up the far side of the slough. This gave me a face—on shot and I could see the horns outside of each of his ears. One shot low in the brisket dropped the deer in its tracks. I crossed the stream in my waders. The size of the whitetail on the other side amazed me. He was an eleven point buck with thick heavy horns and beautiful brow tines!

Gary had heard the shot and came running. We cleaned the deer but left him due to oncoming darkness. I realized the reason I could see him so well as he walked toward me was that the sun was setting behind him. Next morning we took pictures and dragged the deer back to the truck for a return to Colorado. I had a very successful whitetail hunt.

The size of the whitetail on the other side amazed me.
He was an eleven point buck with thick heavy horns
and beautiful brow tines!

High Country Buck Hunt

Every year I look forward to the changing of colors in the mountains. It was especially eventful this year for I had drawn a high country buck permit. Colorado gives some high country buck permits—the hunter can only shoot a mule deer that is four points or more per side—within a wilderness described by the Colorado Division of Wildlife. I was lucky enough to draw one for the Snowmass-Maroon Bells Wilderness area where eight years before I had hunted sheep and had seen many large bucks.

Over the Labor Day weekend Dow Rippy and I took two horses and rode about 16 miles in one day. We scouted the country we were going to hunt the following weekend. We were lucky enough to see ten bighorn rams as well as a small black bear in our circular ride. The day was beautiful and warm and the high country looked magnificent. A few leaves were starting to turn as we made our way out through the aspen.

I had contacted Craig Schultz who had done some bear guiding and had horses to pack in my camp and hunt the following weekend. My horse, Lightning, was not in the best shape. Neither was I from the previous week's ride. I was quite sore but had worked out and soaked in the hot tub long enough to release some of it. It's amazing what happens when you don't ride on a routine basis. The season opened Saturday morning, September 9. Friday morning we were in Glenwood Springs in the middle of a torrential downpour. We were unable to see the area due to the dark cloud cover. We knew the weather would be extremely tough. On the previous sheep hunt it had snowed in September more than once and it was always windy in the high country. We finally decided after the sun came out at 10:00 in the morning to make a break for the area and try to get our camp set up.

We arrived at Snowmass campground at 1:00 in the afternoon. Another front blew in and it rained heavily again. When this didn't lift in 30 minutes, we decided the time was right to take our horses and head for the high country in spite of the weather. The six mile ride out of the East Snowmass trail head was wet, miserable, and cold. The wind was blowing hard and by the time we reached a mile out of the trail head it had started to snow. The horses were surefooted and made their way up the long narrow trail. After two hours we broke out of the timber and into an area where the scrub trees were starting to come back on a reforestation effort after an old fire. Another mile and we passed a sheep camp where two hunters had sheep permits and two other hunters had high country buck permits.

We would set up camp along a long valley just where the trees ended to provide some shelter. We found a good area for the horses to graze along the creek and started setting up our camp in the middle of a snowstorm. The Jansport tent went up fairly easily. We built a large fire which made things a lot better. That evening the wind died and the stars came out. We were hoping that by next morning it would still be clear and the snow would start to melt. We were able to get everything out of our saddlebags and into the tent without getting soaked. Keeping dry is the key factor in staying warm in the high country.

The next morning there was ice in the coffee cups when we awoke. After a quick breakfast we saddled our horses and were ready to go. We headed straight up the trail toward East Snowmass Pass. Approximately two miles out of camp we heard some bugling to our left and noticed a large herd of elk. We continued along the trail and spooked the elk. They had to cross our trail about 100 yards in front of us. It was quite a sight with the snow covered valley and 38 elk parading in front of us. There were six bulls including a heavily horned five point bull who was the master of the herd. They snaked their way up over the ridge and stood skylined before going down to main Snowmass Creek.

We made our way up East Snowmass Pass and reached the top at about 8:30 A.M. We headed down the other side in the fresh snow. The first track we saw was a coyote. Following the trail down into the Willow Lake we noticed fresh deer tracks on the trail. A few minutes later, looking up the ridge to the west we noticed four bucks crossing a rock scree and heading straight toward the top of the mountain. None of the bucks were trophy quality, so we continued on our way. Dropping down into Willow Lake and then into West Willow Basin, we headed along a very steep rocky trail. The snow had melted off the trail since it faced the sun and we slowly made our way back to what is known as Waterfall Basin.

Just before reaching the basin at a small water hole we noticed some movement and a few does ran off. Behind the does, a large buck made his way into the pine trees and headed up into the basin where we were going. We made our way over to the stream and looked at the fresh tracks. Then we rode up a small glasiated side canyon to a point where we had to walk about 200 yards at a 60 degree angle and over a small saddle to get into the large basin. We slowly made our way up over the top. I carried the gun and some sandwiches and Craig carried a backpack with the spotting scope. We reached the top and glassed the basin but found no deer. We made our way down to the point on a short ridge where we could glass over the entire area. By this time the sun was up. We could see green slopes on Sievers Peak, directly across from our area. We laid down, put the spotting scope up, and continued to glass through this area.

About noon we decided Craig would make a circular stalk and I would go out on a point and watch for anything coming my way. As he reached the far side of the basin ten bighorn sheep came out of the trees and made their way over the top. All were ewes and lambs with small rams having only their lamb tips. This was another exciting animal that can be seen during a high country hunt. Craig finished his circle through the trees and came to a small canyon. He kicked out a doe which I could see plainly on the far side of the canyon. I heard a noise just to my left in one of the steep canyons from the point that I was watching. It made two or three loud sounds like rocks moving. I moved toward the sound, but I couldn't see around the corner. Later I found out Craig had kicked out a large buck that had run directly toward me, then up this steep gully. He had shielded himself from me—only 50 yards away!

After getting together, I decided to take the horses to the basin. I climbed back to the top of the area to see if the buck had stayed out on the point where he had climbed. We saw a coyote watching the point where we suspected the deer might be. I climbed back to the top of the mountain and slowly worked my way down—zig-zagging back and forth looking for this large buck. He had given us the slip. I met with Craig around the point of the ridge and we sat down for lunch.

The day was warm after the cold snowy evening. We decided on our strategy for the rest of the day. We were going to go back over East Snowmass Pass. I would climb the ridge between East Snowmass Creek and Main Snowmass Creek and work my way along the ridge while Craig took the three horses back to camp. I would come off the side of the ridge just above camp and make my way down. After lunch we went back over East Snowmass Pass in an uneventful fashion. We took one horse up on the ridge and saw the large basins in which the elk had gone the previous morning. I left the horses with Craig. He headed back for the other two horses and started down the ridge. I sat down and glassed each basin I came upon, for a while. Continually looking in the East Snowmass Creek Basin on the shady side I didn't see any animals. At one spot on a low point in the ridge I could see directly across East Snowmass Creek to the sunlit west facing slope. On picking my glasses up and putting them on the area where the sun was just meeting the vegetation I noticed four bucks. The largest buck was working his way to the left and I could see horns from two miles away! I knew that this deer was worth a closer look. I decided to try to catch Craig before he passed me on the trail on the way back to camp. I bailed off the side of the mountain and made my way down toward the trail. The snow had melted and the ground was soft which made the walking easier especially going downhill. I didn't have a pack to worry about and only my rifle to concern me. Keeping the rifle on the outside shoulder when traversing the hillside made going down easy.

I got to the trail just as Craig got there with the three horses and showed him where the deer were on the side of the hill. There were now only three bucks feeding up high with six does underneath them in a small basin. We hobbled the horses and headed out to a small ridge where we could set up the spotting scope. We glassed for about 30 minutes only seeing the three smaller bucks. The larger buck had fed to the left out of sight. Finally the large buck stood up and we could see he was quite high and completely in velvet. Although I had five trophy mule deer from Colorado, I had none that were totally in velvet. I felt that this was an excellent opportunity for a new trophy.

We watched the deer feed back and forth, unaware of our presence. A few of the does that were closer seemed to know that we were there but the wind was blowing very hard into our faces, so we were fairly sure they had not smelled us. We made plans for the stalk. I would work along the shady ridge over toward the deer in a circular fashion to the right. Craig would sit with the spotting scope and direct me if the deer moved. Most of the time I would be in sight of the deer although I would be in the shade. A small ridge and some scrub trees in the area would shield me the final 200 yards of the stalk.

I started down over the ridge and got in the shade. I worked my way to the right. In about half an hour I was in front of the ridge that concealed the deer. I caught my breath and made my way up over the ridge and into a clump of small scrub trees. They didn't grow very high due to the harsh weather in the area. It was getting late and the sun was setting but the deer were still in the sun which made them easy to see. The large deer was still feeding and had not started to rub his horns as some of the smaller deer had. I found a dead stump in the middle of the clump of trees and used it for a rest. My .300 Weatherby roared and the deer collapsed. He flipped over twice and came to a stop on a small game trail that was approximately 250 yards away.

The shot startled the other deer and they headed up out of the vegetation onto the rock scree portion of the ridge. I thought the deer would run laterally either down the valley or up the valley but they didn't. Much to my surprise as I looked back at the deer there were now four bucks. One was in velvet although not quite as large as the one that had fallen. He had been sleeping among the smaller bucks and jumped up after the shot. They headed straight up and over the ridge into Waterfall Basin where we had been the previous morning. I slowly made my way up to my buck. It was about a 70 degree angle! I found him just where I thought he would be. It's important to spot bare areas or clumps of trees around a fallen animal to give a point of reference as you climb the ridge.

Through all the falling, dragging, turning, and packing my buck
only lost a small area of velvet. He made a *spectacular* trophy.
I now have all *five species* of North American deer.

After cleaning the animal I made my way back to the creek to clean myself and my knife. My scope had hit me between the eyes and left a very nice bruise. I was laying flat on the ground and shooting at about a 60 degree angle uphill. Craig, having seen all the activity through the spotting scope, got the horses and brought them around so we could load the deer on the horse. After dragging the deer downhill 100 yards or so, we were able to get him in the panniers and head back to camp. It was dark by the time we reached the valley floor. The horses did an excellent job on walking the trail back to camp in the dark. The moon was out, but once we hit the trees the last 400-500 yards prior to camp, it was very dark. We relied on the horses to make their way to camp without falling.

The night was clear and cold. We made beef stew over a warm fire and had some coffee which made the evening seem lot more comfortable. We had put in a long day, walking up and down many thousand feet. The sleeping bag really felt good that night... and we soon dozed off until morning. The wind picked up just before we went to bed and had blown in four inches of new snow by morning. September in the high country is always unpredictable.

We packed our camp and got the horses ready to make our way back out. Although we were extremely tired, the two hour ride out was uneventful. The aspens below had turned brilliant yellow and were quite beautiful. Through all the falling, dragging, turning, and packing my buck only lost a small area of velvet. He made a *spectacular* trophy.

I now have all *five species* of North American deer. Deer hunting is very much like hunting sheep. It gets under your skin. And if one sets the rule of not shooting a deer any smaller than one previously shot, it becomes very exciting. I have maintained that tenor throughout my deer hunting days. I am now at the point where it takes an exceptional buck to hang on my wall.

Every fall I still find myself traipsing the hills of Colorado looking for that monster mule deer. If I had time I would also like to upgrade my Coues and Columbian blacktail deer trophies. Most young hunters start by hunting some type of deer. I think this edges in their mind a quality that is hard to forget.

16

The Fifth North American Sheep

After the first of the year, winter time is typically the time we clean guns and watch sports instead of hunting. But I was looking for new species, especially a sheep related species. I had been trying to arrange a free ranging aoudad hunt for the past few years. I finally settled on Steve Jones of Back Country Hunts of Carlsbad, New Mexico. After, I confirmed the fair chase portion of the hunt with previous hunters and reliable references, I booked the hunt for the first of February. We had decided that during the winter the hair on the aoudad would be in prime condition and it would give us a good break from our winter doldrums.

Attending the Safari Club International convention in Reno certainly didn't dampen our enthusiasm for the upcoming hunt. February 1st rolled around as an Arctic cold front crept down from Alaska to the lower 48. It had provided sub-zero weather to Alaska over the past month and looked as though it would do much the same for the lower part of the U.S. My hunting companion, Jerry Bachmann and I left the airport in sub-zero weather. Yet, only two hours later 65 degree temperatures and a small amount of rain greeted us in El Paso, Texas. We rented a car and made the three hour drive south and east to the Sunday House Inn in Alpine, Texas. We arrived at 11:00 P.M. The bed felt good after a long day of traveling.

The next morning we were up at 5:15 to met Steve Jones, the outfitter, and our guide, Barry. After a hearty breakfast at a next-door cafe. We bought our Texas hunting licenses and were ready for the short truck ride to the ranch. Twelve miles south and east of Alpine, Texas, we entered a ranch and drove through a long area of flat ranch land and dry creek beds. We approached two large mountain ranges whose tops were in the fog. We dropped Jerry and Barry off at the lower end and made our way up Old Blue Canyon. They would climb the mountain range and work their way back toward us. We drove to the end of the canyon and glassed each side. No aoudad. After considerable glassing we left the truck and started up the middle ridge between two large east and west canyons. Within about 500 yards, we spotted our first group of 26 aoudad, many of which were large males.

The aoudad, or barbery sheep, are hardy critters that hail from the isolated desert mountains of the Sahara. They were once common in the Ennedi Mountains in northern Chad. Once they roamed a broad belt from Mauretania in Morocco to Egypt and the Sudan; the aoudad is now rare in its native range. Uncontrolled poaching by locals and the military during the numerous revolutions have swept this region and all but exterminated the animal on its home ground.

Called the wild sheep, the aoudad is technically neither a sheep nor a goat. Still it has characteristics of both. In a free ranging state the aoudad counts as one of the 13 sheep for a super slam. To the hunter they are a beautiful trophy animal. A big male may weigh as much as 300 pounds; 250 is not unusual. They are an attractive sandy beige color and sport long silky hair on their chest and the front upper portion of their forelegs. They make a very impressive mount.

Today's hunter in search of an aoudad can rule out Africa. The good news is they have been one of the most successful transplant of exotic animals to the southwestern United States. Both Texas and New Mexico have extensive herds of aoudads. Hunts are available in many different areas. The Big Bend country of Texas provides some of the most exciting and wild country for stalking this animal.

It is a thrill to hunt exotics and they make exceptional trophies. Needless to say the tougher and more sporting, the better the hunt. Steve Jones provided as wild a hunt as I have had for any type of sheep. Glassing the far off ridge, we watched the herd slowly work around some rocky pinnacles and settle down. The aoudad is known for its skittishness and we were not about to show ourselves. Even though they were about a mile away, we could see there were a fair number of trophy males in the group. After feeding around the steep edge, they settled down to feed in what looked like multiple steep small drainages.

There was nothing but air between the aoudad and us, so we decided to work our way up the middle ridge. We would keep out of sight and then try to figure out how to make our stalk from the top down. We didn't know where Jerry and Barry were. We figured by the time we got to the top, they would make their way along the ridge to meet us. After a long slow walk uphill, which reminded me of my desert sheep hunt three years before we topped out. We looked into all the other basins on the back side of Old Blue Mountain. We made our way around the top of the knob to an area above the sheep. The Glass Mountains of west Texas are a true haven for this mountain exotic. We worked our way down the ridge and into position, then set up the spotting scope. The sheep were now approximately 400 yards below us but it was still hard to determine the best ram.

We saw Jerry and Barry coming over the mountain. We dropped out of sight of the sheep and waved furiously to get them to our position. After a few tense minutes they decided to take a look over the front edge. Fortunately they didn't spook the sheep. They finally saw our efforts to get their attention and made their way down the back side of the mountain toward our hiding place. The sheep had settled down. We decided to have lunch and plan our stalk.

We chose a route along a small finger we could hide behind. We could get down to some 200 yards across the canyon from the aoudad. The ridge was entirely rock and afforded us good cover until we got directly across from the sheep. We slowly made our way down the steep shale-like volcanic rock to some dead trees. We could see the canyon below from here. After looking at the sheep through the glasses we determined there were three large rams. The largest ram had laid down.

We had a brief meeting and decided I would shoot first. After my shot, Jerry was to shoot the second largest ram regardless of his position. We were 100 yards above and 200 yards across from the band of sheep. One ram kept looking our way and appeared to be getting nervous. The wind was blowing very strongly uphill—certainly blowing our sound and scent away from the rams. The large ram finally bedded down in a spot that gave me a quartering shot from behind. Jerry worked about 20 yards below me and we both got into position to shoot. The shot was about 275 yards across the canyon and down the slope. In spite of the wind, we felt the 180 grain bullets in our .300 Weatherby magnums would carry.

We both had good rests. I pulled the trigger and saw the large ram flinch. The other rams had not heard my shot because of the wind. They didn't even budge until mine struggled to get up. Jerry's ram stood up and a second shot hit him. It took Jerry one more shot to anchor his animal. Both rams fell over the cliff 20 yards from each other and down the steep slope. Steve and Barry were pleased with our shooting ability. They saw both rams down, with the scope. We started across the canyon to get them. We worked across the steep canyon and over to where the aoudad had fallen. Barry and Steve soon caught up. They were ready to skin and cape out the two large aoudads. Both animals were trophy quality. Mine measured over 30 inches and Jerry's measured more than 27 inches.

It was 4:15 P.M.—the stalk had started at 7:00 in the morning. We had worked nine hours over very rugged terrain to get in position to pull the trigger. This was as satisfying a stalk as I had made on any previous sheep hunt. The aoudads were cleaned and caped. Barry and Steve's backpacks were full as we headed down the steep canyon. It took about an hour to get back to the truck. The going was tedious along the steep terrain.

Barry went for his truck and the two backpacks. Steve, Jerry, and I checked out a canyon in the Glass Mountains where

Steve had seen Javelina. We drove to the head of the canyon again and saw nothing. It was getting late as we turned and

The Aoudad was trophy quality. He measured over 30 inches.

headed back to Alpine. About half way back at about 6:15, we noticed some Javelina at the base of one of the mountains. We hurried across the floor of the canyon to get into position.

The one wild native pig-like animal found in the United States is the Javelina (collared peccary). They range from Mexico into southwestern Texas, southeastern Arizona and southern New Mexico—and can't be found anywhere else in this country. The Javelina averages about 36 inches in length and between 20 and 24 inches in height at the shoulder. A good size animal weighs between 40 and 60 pounds. The basic colors are a grizzled black and gray. There is a dark dorsal stripe on most and almost always a lighter area over the front of the shoulders. The fur is very coarse. This aggressive animal has a short but distinctly pig-like snout, fairly large ears, almost no tail, and dagger-like canines or tusks.

The peccary is an animal of brushy semidesert areas. They prefer to live where the prickly pear grows but can be found in almost any dense thicket. Chaparral or scrub oak suits them well. They like rocky canyons for cover and Old Blue Canyon offers all of this. The peccary is usually part of a band consisting of about six animals, although bands may be as small as three or as large as 25. The band has a limited home range and will stay within it for long periods.

Javalinas are most active during the early morning hours and in the late afternoon. During the fierce heat of the midday sun they bed down in dense brush. They den in hollow logs or in hollows in the ground. Despite his strength and his formidable tusks, the peccary has enemies. The jaguar, cougar, bobcat, coyote, and wolf all take their toll—but not a very large one. Although he has poor eyesight the peccary has exceptionally keen hearing and a sense of smell that would put a bloodhound to shame. Javelina are quick to sense danger and will usually retreat. Where we had seen only two from the road, by the time we had crossed the canyon floor and got up against the hill we found nine. We picked two of the largest and had our second trophies. After taking pictures we packed and headed back to Alpine, Texas.

Temperatures during this time of year range from a low of about 40 degrees to a high of about 60 degrees. It was dark by the time we made Alpine. Barry and Steve caped and skinned

Javalinas are most active during the early morning hours
and in the late afternoon. During the fierce heat
of the midday sun they bed down in dense brush.

while Jerry and I cleaned our rifles. The next morning Steve and Barry completed the caping while Jerry and I packed the meat. The Alaskan storm moved in and temperatures dropped into the teens. The fog was so thick you couldn't see your hand in front of your face. Although we had set aside four days for this hunt we were lucky to complete it in two days, for the cold and foggy weather would have made hunting very difficult. Jerry and I drove back to El Paso, where the weather was still fair. Then we flew into the sub-zero cold that engulfed Denver.

Anyone interested in breaking the winter doldrums with a fair chase hunt should consider the challenge of going after aoudad in west Texas.

17

Brooks Range Grizzly — the Second Try

It had been eight years since I had hunted for bear in the spring. I decided it was time for a second hunt. I'd heard about an Alaskan guide named Johnny Walker through my friend, Jerry Criswell, who lived in Carbondale, Colorado. He knew Don and was aware I had gone after a grizzly before without success. He stated that Johnny had a terrific grizzly population. After talking to John and seeing some of his pictures I made ready for the hunt in early May.

The weekend before we left we had a Safari Club International board meeting in New Orleans that I attended. On Sunday morning at 6:45 A.M. I boarded a Chicago bound plane with some board members who were returning to Michigan. Vern Edewaard, the newly elected president of Safari Club International, was returning to Alaska to continue a brown bear hunt, interrupted by the meeting. During the flight to Chicago we discussed committee procedures as well as goals for Vern's presidential year.

Spring hunting is a completely different hunting experience than hunting in the fall when the leaves are still on the trees and most of the antlered game is in the rut. In the spring there is an awakening of the northern conscience. The snow is just melting, the animals are losing their winter coats, and the birds are returning north to nest. This was evident in my previous trip to British Columbia.

The flight to Anchorage was uneventful. After I saw all the trophies in the Clarion Hotel just next to the Anchorage Airport, I was *ready* for my hunt. The next day we boarded a 737 to Kotzebue, Alaska. We stopped at Nome on the Seward Peninsula and were awed by some of the old mining artifacts. We crossed the peninsula to Kotzebue, which sits on a small peninsula just underneath the Brooks Range. Two large rivers, the Noatak and Kobuk, enter a sound right next to Kotzebue. Kotzebue is the hub of the Brooks Range and, although there are only 2500 people, it has a major airport. The bay was still frozen but the runway was clear as we landed in Kotzebue. After meeting Johnny Walker, we transferred my gear, purchased licenses, and packed his Super Cub as tight as possible. The Cub was on the bay where the snow had melted down, but there was still a good ice coverage. It had skis.

As we took off I noticed all the surrounding ground was pretty brown. The snow had melted and the weather was terrific. We flew east and then north to the Omar River and climbed over a small pass entering into the Noatak Basin. Flying over the pass we saw a 6½ - 7 foot grizzly lying on a caribou kill at the head of the Omar River. Once over the pass and into the Noatak Watershed the ground cover was completely different. Here the river was mostly open, although there were still parts that were frozen solid across and covered with snow. About 200 yards in either direction from the river the ground was snow covered.

We landed on a snow covered lake by a cabin his dad had established years before. Nelson Walker was one of the premier polar bear guides of the time. We put our gear in the cabin and sighted our rifles. That night the warmth of the cabin felt wonderful as the cold settled into the valley.

In the bright early morning dawn of the next day we were off. Johnny had a packboard and I carried a daypack with lunches. We headed west on the Noatak River. The tundra area right along the river was nearly free of snow although still quite wet. It made walking difficult. Our Sorels really came in handy. There was still snow on all the north facing

We landed on a snow covered lake by a cabin his dad
had established years before. Nelson Walker was one
of the premier polar bear guides of the time.

That night the warmth of the cabin felt wonderful
as the cold settled into the valley.

slopes, the side hills, and any place that was shaded. We walked about 15 miles west and saw another 6½-7 foot grizzly feeding in the willows along the small lake. After lunch, we spotted still another feeding on a caribou kill. The vastness of the country in the Brooks Range was quite a sight. While flying in, the day before, we had seen many moose and caribou along the river bottom. Dall sheep were along the mountains behind camp. Since it stayed light until about 1:00 in the morning we hunted until 5 P.M. before heading back to camp. We returned to camp tired and hungry. A warm meal was waiting and the ability to dry out was welcomed.

The next morning we were down the river again glassing both sides. This time we saw more moose in the willows as the snow continued to melt around us. We took a side river out of the Noatak, walked for a few miles before the snow got too deep and turned around and headed back home. When we got to within a few miles of camp, we came to an area we had seen from the other side of the river. It sported some small hills which had lusher grass than other areas. Coming over the first hill we noticed movement 200 yards away. We sat down, took our backpacks off, and got our glasses out.

Feeding close to a caribou kill a 7½-8 foot blonde grizzly was making its way along the grass eating the green shoots that were sprouting.

We watched him through the glasses for a long time. His coat was full with frosted tips and he had dark paws. It was early in the hunt but we had to consider that the weather might change. This certainly was a trophy class grizzly so we watched the bear some more. We took some pictures of him feeding and decided he was better than we had thought. We decided to try a stalk.

We had three small areas to hide behind as we approached the bear. The wind was blowing in our face so we knew he wouldn't smell us. We crept slowly from one small hump of ground to another until we came to an area where the bear should be about 75 yards in front of us. We crawled up over the last hump—no bear. We laid there for a minute and the bear fed around a small little hill that had hidden him from us.

We took some more pictures and decided he was the one.

I laid the Weatherby across my hat and fired one shot. The bear fell to all fours. We were sure he was going to get up and run so I put another shell in the chamber. There was no movement. We made our way slowly over to him, came up behind him, and nudged him with the end of the barrel. The bear wasn't breathing. Weatherby anesthesia had done the job.

We took pictures, skinned the bear out, and put him in a bag. Johnny put him on his packboard. The return to camp through the wet ground surrounding the Noatak River was much easier than the nights before! We celebrated with a great dinner and laid the hide out to cool overnight.

The next day Johnny worked on the hide while I took my camera and walked about two miles to the closest ridge. We had spotted some Dall sheep through a scope and I thought I'd get closer to take some pictures. As I made my way up close to the rock scree edge of the mountain, much to my surprise, the Dall sheep fed toward me. One of my greatest thrills in the wild was watching a full curl dall ram walk to within 20 yards of me during this camera stalk. Although I was only using a camera it may have been more exciting than if I had a rifle. I returned to find Johnny had the bear completely skinned out and the skull ready to boil.

The next six days were some of my most enjoyable in the wild. We took boat trips up rivers. I photographed Dall sheep, moose, and caribou on the move, and saw wolves from the super cub. I actually saw spring come alive in northern Alaska! Much to my delight the waterfowl were back again in unbelievable numbers, including swans nesting in the area. On the fifth day we moved camp from the high reaches of the Brooks Range down to the lower river camp. Here there were even more waterfowl. And the fishing was unbelievable.

Thus ended my quest for all 24 huntable species of the North American 27 that are legal to import into the United States. It had taken me 12 years to put them in my trophy room.

Three more species not allowed to be imported, are the jaguar, polar bear, and walrus. It is legal to hunt jaguar in Mexico and South America, polar bear in Canada, and walrus in Canada. But the Marine Mammal Act does not allow the import of any of them into the United States. This ban has been in effect since 1968.

The jaguar is on the CITES appendix 1 list which allows no striped or spotted cats other than the leopard. Some day in the future, when the huntable population again return to North America, I hope to be able to add these three species to my North American Trophy wall.

Appendix I

Fish and Game Departments

United States

Alabama Department of Conservation and Natural Resources
Division of Game and Fish
64 N. Union Street
Montgomery, AL 36130
PH: 205-261-3465

Alaska Department of Fish and Game
Division of Wildlife Conservation
Box 3-2000
Juneau, AK 99804
PH: 907-465-4190

Arizona Game and Fish Department
2222 W. Greenway Rd.
Phoenix, AZ 85023
PH: 602-942-3000

Arkansas Game and Fish Commission
No. 2 Natural Resources Dr.
Little Rock, AR 72205
PH: 501-223-6300

California Department of Fish and Game
Wildlife Management Division
1416 Ninth Street
Sacramento, CA 95814
PH: 916-445-3531

Colorado Division of Wildlife
6060 Broadway
Denver, CO 80216
PH: 303-297-1192

Connecticut Department of Environmental Protection
Wildlife Bureau
165 Capitol Ave., Room 254
Hartford, CT 06106
PH: 203-566-4683

Delaware Department of Natural Resources and Environmental Control
Division of Fish and Wildlife
89 Kings Highway, POB 2402
Dover, DE 29903
PH: 302-736-5297

Florida Game and Fresh Water Fish Commission
620 S. Meridian Street
Tallahassee, FL 32399-1600
PH: 904-488-4676

Georgia Department of Natural Resources
Game and Fish Division
205 Butler Street S.E., #1362
Atlanta, GA 30334
PH: 404-656-3530

Hawaii Department of Land and Natural Resources
Division of Forestry and Wildlife
1151 Punchbowl Street
Honolulu, HI 96813
PH: 808-548-8850

Idaho Department of Fish and Game
600 S. Walnut Street, POB 25
Boise, ID 83707
PH: 208-334-3700

Illinois Department of Conservation
Lincoln Tower Plaza
524 S. Second Street
Springfield, IL 62701
PH: 217-782-6384

Indiana Department of Natural Resources
Division of Fish and Wildlife
607 State Office Building
Indianapolis, IN 46294
PH 317-232-4080

Iowa Conservation Commission
Wallace State Office Building
Des Moines, IA 50319
PH: 515-281-5918

Kansas Department of Wildlife and Parks
Route 2, Box 54A
Pratt, KS 67124
PH: 316-672-5911

Kentucky Department of Fish and Wildlife Resources
Frankfort, KY 40601
PH: 502-564-4336

Louisiana Department of Wildlife and Fisheries, I. & E.
Division
POB 98000
Baton Rough, LA 70898-9000
PH: 504-765-2916

Maine Department of Inland Fisheries and Wildlife
284 State Street
State House Station 41
Augusta, ME 04333
PH: 207-289-2871

Maryland Forest, Park, and Wildlife Service
Tawes State Office Building
Annapolis, MD 21401
PH: 301-974-3195

Massachusetts Division of Fisheries and Wildlife
100 Cambridge Street
Boston, MA 02202
PH: 617-727-2864

Michigan Wildlife Division
Michigan Department of Natural Resources
POB 30028
Lansing, MI 48909
PH: 517-373-1263

Minnesota Department of Natural Resources
Division of Fish and Wildlife
POB 7, DNR Building 500 Lafayette
St. Paul, MN 55155
PH: 612-296-6157

Mississippi Department of Wildlife Conservation
Southport Mall, POB 451
Jackson, MS 39205
PH: 313-751-4115

Montana Department of Fish, Wildlife and Parks
1420 E. Sixth Ave.
Helena, MT 59601
PH: 406-444-2535

Nebraska Game and Parks Commission
2200 N. 33rd Street, POB 30370
Lincoln, NE 68503
PH: 402-464-0641

Nevada Department of Wildlife
1100 Valley Road, POB 10678
Reno, NV 89520
PH: 702-789-0500

New York Department of Environmental Conservation
Fish and Wildlife Division
50 Wolf Road
Albany, NY 12233
PH: 518-457-5400

New Hampshire Fish and Game Department
2 Hazen Drive
Concord, NH 03301
PH: 603-271-3421

New Jersey Department of Environmental Protection
Division of Fish, Game and Wildlife
CN-400
Trenton, NJ 08625
PH: 609-292-2965

New Mexico Department of Game and Fish
State Capitol Villagra Building
Santa Fe, NM 87503
PH: 505-827-7882

North Dakota Game and Fish Department
100 N. Bismarck Expressway
Bismarck, ND 58501
PH: 701-221-6300

North Carolina Wildlife Resources Commission
512 N. Salisbury Street
Raleigh, NC 27611
PH: 919-733-3391

Oklahoma Department of Wildlife Conservation
1801 N. Lincoln, POB 53465
Oklahoma City, OK 73105
PH: 405-521-3851

Ohio Department of Natural Resources
Division of Wildlife
1500 Dublin Road
Columbus, OH 43215

Oregon Department of Fish and Wildlife
506 S.W. Mill Street
Portland, OR 97207
PH: 503-229-5551

Pennsylvania Game Commission
2001 Elmerton Ave.
Harrisburg, PA 17110-9797
PH: 717-787-6286

Rhode Island Department of Environmental Management
Division of Fish and Wildlife
Government Center, Tower Hill Road
Wakefield, RI 02879
PH: 401-789-3094

South Carolina Wildlife and Marine Resources Department
POB 167
Columbia, SC 29202
PH: 803-734-3888

South Dakota Department of Game, Fish, and Parks
Anderson Building
Pierre, SD 57501
PH: 605-773-3485

Tennessee Wildlife Resources Agency
POB 40747
Nashville, TN 37204
PH: 625-360-0500

Texas Parks and Wildlife Department
4200 Smith School Road
Austin, TX 78744
PH: 512-389-4800

Utah Division of Wildlife Resources
2596 W. North Temple
Salt Lake City, UT 84116
PH: 801-533-9333

Vermont Fish and Wildlife Department
Waterbury, VT 05676
PH: 802-244-7331

Virginia Department of Game and Inland Fisheries
4010 W. Broad Street, POB 11104
Richmond, VA 23230-1104
PH: 804-367-1000

Washington Department of Wildlife
600 Capitol Way N.
Olympia, WA 98504
PH: 206-753-5700

West Virginia Wildlife Resources Division
1800 Washington Street, East
Charleston, WV 25305
PH: 304-348-2771

Wisconsin Bureau of Wildlife Management
POB 7921
Madison, WI 53707
PH: 608-266-1877

Wyoming Game and Fish Department
Cheyenne, WY 82002
PH: 307-777-7735

Mexico

Mexico Wildlife Advisory Services
POB 76132 Department HM-9
Los Angeles, CA 90076
PH: 213-385-9311

Canada

Alberta Forestry Lands and Wildlife
Fish and Wildlife Division
9920 108th Street
Edmonton, Alberta T5K 2G6
PH: 403-427-3590

British Columbia Wildlife Branch
Ministry of Environment
Parliament Buildings
Victoria, British Columbia V8V 1X5

Manitoba Department of Natural Resources
1495 St. James Street, Box 22
Winnipeg, Manitoba R3H 0W9
PH: 204-945-6784

New Brunswick Department of Natural Resources
Fish and Wildlife Branch
POB 6000
Fredericton, New Brunswick E3B 5H1
PH: 506-453-2433

Newfoundland Department of Culture, Recreation, and Youth
Wildlife Division
POB 4750
St. John's, Newfoundland A1C 5T7
PH: 709-576-2815

Northwest Territories Department of Renewable Resources
Government of Northwest Territories
Box 1320
Yellowknife, Northwest Territories X1A 2L9
PH: 403-920-8716

Nova Scotia Department of Land and Forests
POB 698
Halifax, Nova Scotia B3J 2T9
PH: 902-424-4297

Ontario Ministry of Natural Resources
Public Information Center
Parliament Building
Toronto, Ontario M7A 1W3
PH: 416-965-4251

Prince Edward Island Fish and Wildlife Division
Department of Community Affairs
POB 2000
Charlottetown, Prince Edward Island, C1A 7N8

Quebec Department of Loisir, Chasse, et Peche
150 Street Cyrille E.
Quebec City, Quebec G1R 4Y1
PH: 418-643-2464

Saskatchewan *Tourism Saskatchewan*
2130 11th Ave.
Regina, Saskatchewan S4P 3V7
PH: 1-800-667-7191

Yukon Territory Department of Renewable Resources
Fish and Wildlife Branch
Box 2703
Whitehorse, Yukon Territory Y1A 2C6
PH: 403-667-5811

Appendix II

Species

COMMON NAME	SCIENTIFIC NAME
black bear	*Ursus americanus americanus*
grizzly bear	*Ursus arctos*
Alaskan brown bear	*Ursus arctos middendorffi*
polar bear	*Ursus maritimus*
jaguar	*Felis onca*
cougar or mountain lion	*Felis concolor*
Atlantic walrus	*Odobenus rosmarus rosmarus*
Pacific walrus	*Odobenus rosmarus divergens*
American elk (Wapiti)	*Cervus elaphus nelsoni*
Roosevelt's elk	*Cervus elaphus rooso*
mule deer	*Odocoileus hemionus*
Columbia blacktail deer	*Odocoileus hemionus columbianus*
Sitka blacktail deer	*Odocoileus hemionus sitkensis*
whitetail deer	*Odocoileus virginianus*
Coues' whitetail deer	*Odocoileus virginianus couesi*
Canada moose	*Alces alces americana andersoni*

Alaska-Yukon moose	*Alces alces gigas*
Wyoming or Shiras moose	*Alces alces shirasi*
mountain caribou	*Rangifer tarandus caribou*
woodland caribou	*Rangifer tarandus caribou*
barren ground caribou	*Rangifer tarandus granti*
Central Canada B.G. caribou	*Rangifer tarandus groenlandicus*
Quebec-Labrador caribou	*Rangifer tarandus caribou*
pronghorn	*Antilocapra americana*
buffalo	*Bison bison*
Rocky Mountain goat	*Oreamnos americanus*
musk ox	*Ovibos moschatus*
bighorn sheep	*Ovis canadensis canadensis*
desert sheep	*Ovis canadensis nelsoni*
Dall's sheep	*Ovis dalli dalli*
Stone's sheep	*Ovis dalli stonei*

Index

*Give the Gift of Hunting Adventure to Your
Friends and Colleagues!*

ORDER FORM

YES, I want _____ copies of *Walk With The Eagles* at $30.00 each, plus $3 shipping per book. (Colorado residents please include $2.10 state sales tax.) Canadian orders must be accompanied by a postal money order in U.S. funds. Allow 30 days for delivery.

☐ Check/money order enclosed ● Charge my ☐ VISA ☐ MC

Name _____ Phone _____

Address _____

City/State/Zip _____

Card # _____ Expires _____

Signature _____

**Check your leading bookstore or call
your credit card order to
(303) 945-6533**

Please make your check payable and return to:

Roaring Fork Press
P. O. Box 563
Glenwood Springs, CO 81602
